The
Political Economy of
Deregulation
Interest Groups
in the Regulatory Process

Roger G. Noll and Bruce M. Owen

American Enterprise Institute for Public Policy Research
Washington and London

Acknowledgments

We are grateful to many at AEI and CBS for suggestions that have undoubtedly improved the work. William Lilley III and George Vradenburg III at CBS and Jack Meyer and Marvin Kosters at AEI were especially helpful. Robert Crandall, Joseph Kalt, and Ken Baseman made significant contributions to chapter 1; Ken Baseman and Peter Greenhalgh were indispensable to the drafting of chapters 2 and 3. Henry Grabowski generously reviewed portions of the manuscript. Paul Gottlieb provided excellent research assistance. The individual authors of each chapter remain, of course, responsible for the content of what they have written, and the editors for the coherence, if any, of the whole.

Library of Congress Cataloging in Publication Data

Noll, Roger G.
   The political economy of deregulation.

   (AEI studies ; 379)
   Includes bibliographical references.
   1.   Industry and state—United States—Case
studies.   2.   Trade regulation—United States—
Case studies.   I.   Owen, Bruce M.   II.   Title.
III.   Title: Deregulation.   IV.   Series.
HD3616.U47N64   1983   338.973   83-2638
ISBN 0-8447-3520-5
ISBN 0-8447-3519-1 (pbk.)

3 5 7 9 10 8 6 4 2

Printed in the United States of America

The
Political Economy of
Deregulation

Contents

Preface

This book has two basic themes. First, regulation itself benefits certain firms at the expense of others, thereby creating and destroying the very interest groups that participate in debates on deregulation. Second, debates about regulatory reform exhibit common properties that, when recognized, can help sort out the public interest from the cacophony of self-interest that surrounds it.

A variety of current regulatory reform controversies are analyzed in this volume along with more detailed case studies of deregulation during the 1970s. While several areas of federal regulation are highlighted, special emphasis is placed on regulatory reform in network broadcasting. The Federal Communications Commission is currently considering a proposal to deregulate certain aspects of broadcast network behavior. Much of the material in this book was initially developed under a commission to the editors from CBS Inc. to help people understand this proposal against a backdrop of the great deregulation debates of the past decade. The study was intended to illustrate how the role of special interest groups and the public interest can be quite similar from one regulatory reform dispute to another, despite widely varying settings. Although each new regulatory dispute may appear unique, this book presents some of the common elements running through regulatory reform controversies.

It became apparent as the study progressed that, if its conclusions were valid, they would necessarily have application not only to the relatively narrow issues in the regulation of network broadcasting, but also to many other current regulatory reform controversies. It was the general applicability of the analysis that made the study of interest to the American Enterprise Institute. Accordingly, the original material has been extended, generalized, and edited under AEI's aegis and direction.

Throughout this book we focus on deregulation, but this is really a shorthand word that stands not only for the relaxation and removal of regulation, but also for its reform. The term "deregulation," as we use it, includes regulatory reform efforts designed to place greater reliance on market forces to serve consumers: to *improve* regulation by reducing the costs of achieving desired regulatory goals. Outright withdrawal of regulation has been proposed in common carrier transportation and in other areas, while in the health, safety, and broadcasting areas most current proposals involve reform, not complete removal of regulation.

While the examples and case studies in this book are drawn almost exclusively from federal experience under regulation, a great deal of regulation also takes place at the state and local levels. We believe that the lessons to be learned from the federal experience with deregulation are equally applicable to such areas as state insurance and utility regulation, cable television franchising, occupational licensure, taxicab regulation, and the many other attempts by states and cities to regulate economic behavior.

ROGER G. NOLL
BRUCE M. OWEN

PART ONE

1
Introduction:
The Agenda for Deregulation

Regulation is a peculiarly American institution, though all nations use political and legal processes to constrain the economic activities of their citizens. The most common method of implementing such policies in other countries is to give government officials great direct authority. Many governments nationalize important industries or set up a controlling bureaucracy that has far more power than the typical American regulatory agency.

American regulation is a reflection of the democratic and egalitarian principles held by the Founding Fathers, especially their fear of centralized government power. Its organizing principle is that decisions should be based upon objective analysis in a process that allows people who are likely to be affected by the decision to have their views heard and considered. Elaborate rules regarding rights of participation, the evidence pertaining to a decision, and the statutory basis for a policy action have developed to serve this principle.

Like many legal processes, regulation in America seeks to base decisions on objective facts, principles of equity, and the public interest, but does so in a decision-making environment that is populated primarily by advocates of particular economic interests. For the most part, participants in the regulatory process are motivated by their economic stakes in the decision, and as a result their behavior in the process—the kinds of evidence and arguments that they will produce—is quite predictable.[1]

During the decade of the 1970s, numerous federal regulatory policies were reexamined with an eye toward major reform and often complete deregulation (see table 1–1). The passage late in 1982 of legislation to deregulate intercity bus service is but the most recent in a series of policy moves to free competitive forces from federal supervision. Stock brokers' fees, railroads, trucks, airlines, petroleum, cable television, radio stations, air cargo service, savings and loan institutions, banks, securities issuers, and other industries have, to varying

degrees, been deregulated since 1974. These industries obviously
have different structures and have had different sorts of regulation

TABLE 1–1
MAJOR DEREGULATORY INITIATIVES, 1971–1982

Year	Deregulatory Initiative
1971	Transportation deregulation (proposed)
	FCC: Specialized common carrier decision
1972	FCC: Domestic satellite open skies policy
1975	SEC: Abolition of fixed brokerage fees
	Trucking deregulation (proposed)
	Banking deregulation (proposed)
	Airline deregulation (proposed)
1976	Railroad Revitalization and Reform Act
1977	Air Cargo Deregulation Act
1978	Airline Deregulation Act
	Natural Gas Policy Act
	OSHA: Standards revocation
	EPA: Emissions trading policy
1979	FCC: Deregulation of satellite earth stations
1980	Motor Carrier Reform Act
	Household Goods Transportation Act
	Staggers Rail Act
	Depository Institutions Deregulation and Monetary Control Act
	International Air Transportation Competition Act
	FCC: Deregulation of cable television
	FCC: Deregulation of customer premises equipment and enhanced services
1981	Decontrol of Crude Oil and Refined Petroleum Products (Executive Order)
	Federal Reserve Board: Truth in lending simplification
	NHTSA: Auto industry regulatory relief package
	FCC: Deregulation of radio
1982	Bus Regulatory Reform Act
	Garn–St Germain Depository Institution Act
	FCC: Deregulation of resale and transponders

NOTE: FCC = Federal Communications Commission; SEC = Securities and Exchange Commission; OSHA = Occupational Safety and Health Administration; EPA = Environmental Protection Agency; NHTSA = National Highway Traffic Safety Administration.

applied to them, and so required separate analyses to sustain the case for reform. Nevertheless, the deregulation debate in each case followed predictable lines.

The deregulation debates continue. One major issue is whether to repeal certain regulations of the Federal Communications Commission (FCC) that constrain the business operations of the three national television broadcast networks.[2] It was this issue that provided the original motivation for this study. The FCC rules were adopted a decade ago on the basis of a record compiled largely in the late 1950s and early 1960s. The rules restrict the ability of the networks to acquire certain valuable rights in the television programs that they air. The networks are on one side of this debate. On the other side are the major Hollywood studios that produce and license television programs to the networks and distribute programs in syndication.

Because deregulation of the television networks involves the media, the political debate has been bathed in publicity. Even though the interests and issues may be no less parochial, network deregulation has received more media attention than many of the other important regulatory policy debates, such as those involving the Clean Air Act or natural gas prices. Yet the debate is likely to be carried out in a vacuum, as if this were the first rather than merely the latest proposal to deregulate an important industry.

It is our thesis that useful insights can be gained from a general understanding of the political economy of deregulation and from taking a broad view of the history of regulation itself. Regulatory regimes, whether in airlines, banking, or broadcasting, have much in common. Each tends to create (and to destroy) groups with special economic interests. The views and arguments of these groups on the question of deregulation are rooted in their own interests. The debate about network deregulation, and other future deregulation debates, will be more enlightened if the positions of the parties and their arguments are not viewed in isolation, but are instead seen as part of a long history of regulatory policy, broadly defined.

The discussion of the regulatory process in the following seven chapters is based largely on this interest group "model." An understanding of the model and of its value in predicting behavior is useful, perhaps most useful to regulators in finding ways to rise above its predictions. The last chapter of this book introduces these more normative concerns and shows that while the interest group model is descriptive of forces at work in the policy process, it need not—indeed, should not—determine the outcome of the regulatory process.

The problem of regulators is to identify a general public interest in a process that is populated largely by interest groups pursuing narrow

5

aims. We recognize that the public interest is an elusive concept, and we do not propose to offer a comprehensive definition of it. Nevertheless, an important aspect of the public interest is to advance the interests of members of society acting in their roles as consumers, and to do so in a manner that promotes economic efficiency. Every citizen has numerous interests, according to occupation, industry of employment, residency, nature of principal investments, political orientation, important social relationships, and pattern of consumption expenditures. A principal insight of the interest group theory of regulatory processes is that some aspects of a citizen's interests are more likely to be effectively represented than others. The task of the regulator is to work out, for each case, the biases that are likely to emerge from the patterns of participation in the regulatory process.

Organization of This Study

This first chapter provides the reader with a brief survey of some current deregulation controversies. We include a summary description of the issues and the stakes the various interest groups have in them. The idea is not in this brief space to analyze in any depth the particular pros and cons of each deregulatory proposal. Our intent is instead to motivate the discussion that follows, in chapter 2, of the interactive role of interest groups and regulators and, in chapter 3, of the types of arguments used by interest groups to defend their positions.

In chapter 2 we explore the political and economic origins of interest groups, their recognition in the federal system by the Founding Fathers, and the relationship between economic regulation and the representation of interest groups in the policy process. Numerous examples from a variety of regulatory arenas are used to illustrate our general analysis of the role of interest groups in regulatory policy.

Chapter 3 provides a survey of the arguments that have been used by opponents of deregulation. Regardless of the regulatory policy in question, groups that have a vested interest in continued regulation make predictable arguments about cross-subsidization and predictions of destructive competition, excessive risk, and harm to consumers. To the extent possible, we comment on the evidence that has become available in these industries since deregulation that bears on these predictions. Such arguments and predictions will inevitably be made in future deregulation debates. Arguments arising from self-interest are not necessarily invalid, but an assessment of the validity of these arguments in other industries can shed light on how to assess their validity in current deregulation debates.

Chapters 4 through 8 contain detailed case studies of particular deregulation episodes, both completed and ongoing. In chapter 4, Andrew Carron examines the effort to reform or to dismantle the constraints that federal regulators have placed on the banking system. Robert Crandall reviews, in chapter 5, the fascinating convergence of environmental and coal-producing interests that led to the 1977 Clean Air Act Amendments. In chapter 6, Joseph Kalt explores the special interest groups that opposed deregulation of the energy industry in the aftermath of the 1973 oil embargo. Finally, in chapters 7 and 8, two highly distinguished economists and former regulators review the actual experience with deregulation in two traditional fields: Marcus Alexis, former commissioner of the Interstate Commerce Commission (ICC), examines deregulation of surface transportation, and Alfred Kahn, former chairman of the Civil Aeronautics Board (CAB), writes about deregulation of the airlines.

Chapter 9 sums up the lessons learned and attempts to generalize beyond the interest group model. This is necessary because it would otherwise be difficult to say why, in at least some cases, the interest group model does not fully explain events—why, for example, airline or trucking deregulation eventually took place despite interest group pressures. We do not understand this political process as well as we understand the essentially economic model of interest group formation. What we do know is that any policy maker considering deregulation must understand the economic basis of interest groups, or else risk giving undue weight to a number of illegitimate arguments.

The balance of this first chapter is devoted to a survey of some major current regulatory reform controversies. There are several reasons for doing this. The first is simply to motivate the discussion in chapter 2 of the interest group model of regulatory policy making. The second is to show how this analysis can be relevant to current policy issues, most of which remain undecided. The third is to begin to demonstrate that apparently unrelated deregulation debates, often conducted in isolation from each other, in fact have much in common. We begin with the FCC's network financial interest and syndication rules.

Network Television Deregulation

The network syndication and financial interest rules impose restrictions on the ability of the three broadcast networks to acquire certain financial interests in the programs that they buy for network exhibition and on their ability to participate in the syndication business.[3] The rules apply only to broadcast networks (that is, ABC, CBS, and NBC).

They do not apply to their competitors, such as the major studios in their roles either as financiers of television program production or as syndicators, or to cable networks, or to potential competitors, such as COMSAT's recently authorized direct broadcast satellite system. The rules are opposed by the broadcast networks, for they restrict the networks' freedom of action. The rules are generally supported by the major movie studios, who supply most of the series programming purchased by the networks and who are given a favored market position by the restrictions these rules place on important former competitors. Although not prominent among the original proponents of the rules, the major Hollywood studios soon became the principal opponents of deregulation. The rules are also supported by program syndicators who are sheltered from the potential competition of the networks as syndicators.

While the studios and the networks are the central antagonists, there are other important groups with less well-defined, homogeneous, or articulated interests, such as independent producers of television shows, television stations of various kinds, and advertisers. Finally, and most important, there are viewers. The effect on the viewing public presumably ought to constitute the basis for any decision to deregulate. The FCC, as the guardian of the public's interest, must weigh the arguments of interest groups as to the positive effects—if any—of regulation on viewers, while remaining indifferent to arguments concerning the effects on the interest groups themselves.

We cannot in this brief space attempt to analyze in any depth the economic effects of the rules that the networks want repealed. Such an analysis has been provided already by the special network inquiry staff of the FCC.[4] But in order to connect the issues in network regulation to the interest group analysis that forms the heart of this book, we will provide a summary of the economic analysis of the effects of the FCC rules.

The production of television programs is risky because the popularity of a program, and hence its effectiveness in generating advertising revenues, is highly unpredictable. One way to cope with risks is to pool them—that is, to hold several risky assets in the expectation that good fortune on some will balance bad luck on others. This is the theory behind investing in a portfolio of different investments rather than putting all of one's wealth in a single asset.

Networks are in a position to pool risks by investing in a portfolio of programs. Before the syndication and financial interest rules, any producer with a creative idea could seek financing from the networks or the movie studios and in exchange sell syndication rights and financial interests. Producers, especially small ones, typically want to sell these rights. With one or only a few programs over which to spread the risks of failure, small producers are unable efficiently to bear such risks. Therefore, one would expect a mutually advantageous sale of the rights having the most uncertain value to larger entities (such as networks) that are in a better position to bear risks. Because of the rules, small producers cannot engage in such agreements with the networks.

The imposition of the rules left small program producers unable to use the networks as a means of reducing their risks. As a consequence, motion picture studios soon became the primary source of funds for financing the production of television series. The studios began to negotiate financial arrangements with program producers that paralleled the old program producer contracts with networks.

The increased role of motion picture studios in spreading the risks of program production has several important economic ramifications. First, it illustrates that the basic form of the old agreements with networks to provide financing in return for a partial sale of rights has continued to play an important role in the industry, but now with different sources of financing. Obviously these arrangements were not purely a manifestation of some special market power that was possessed by networks.

Second, the rules that required the elimination of the networks from their risk-spreading role may remove one of the cheapest methods of spreading risks, by introducing an economically unnecessary middleman. To the extent that networks, because they acquire many programs or are in possession of useful information about potential program success, are able to bear the risks of program failure more efficiently than the movie studios, one would expect the costs of program production to be increased by the rule. Moreover, three-way negotiations about program production and distribution are likely to be more expensive than bilateral negotiations.

Third, the elimination of the networks as sources of risk capital for independent producers may reduce program financing competition for the established motion picture studios. Other things equal, this could produce lower revenues to program talent for financial interest and syndication rights because three important bidders for those rights have been eliminated from competition.

Fourth, by forcing new entrants to the programming industry to obtain financing through a shorter list of established program producers, the rules could be expected to raise entry barriers into program production. By eliminating more efficient bearers of risk (networks), the rules will raise the cost of capital to new or potential entrants in program production. All current producers could be expected to like this aspect of the rules.

Fifth, because network entertainment series programming is a riskier undertaking than many other types of programming, the rules will tend to increase concentration among suppliers of prime-time series programs. The major movie studios may well control a larger fraction of this business than they did before the rules, because they are better able to bear risks than their smaller competitors.

Sixth, the rules reduce the number of competitors, or potential competitors, in syndication markets. Barring the networks from this activity has the effect of making the market potentially less efficient.

The rules have additional effects, unrelated to risk bearing, on the positions of networks and their competitors. The rules effectively partition the entertainment business into segments. Competition across segments is hampered by the rules. The rules restrain the three major networks from acquiring certain valuable rights. Therefore, cable networks, such as Home Box Office (HBO), and other potential entrants into over-the-air network broadcasting, such as syndicators, perceive that the barriers to entry into network broadcasting have been increased by the rules. If they were to enter over-the-air network broadcasting, they could reasonably expect the FCC to expand the rules to cover them. Thus, entry into this kind of broadcasting would force them to give up valuable rights that they currently find desirable to acquire.

The rules clearly place the networks at a competitive disadvantage to other forms of program distribution in today's rapidly changing home video marketplace. The rules reduce the ability of networks to compete for programming with other program distributors. A considerable amount of jockeying among movie houses, networks, and other programmers and distributors is currently occurring as new media develop and new distribution patterns for programming are formed. It would not be surprising to find that the firms competing with networks to distribute programs to new media are comfortable with the constraints the rules place on the networks' ability to compete.

The movie studios and the networks are taking fairly predictable positions on elimination of the financial interest and syndication rules. In many different areas, the ability of networks to compete with movie studios, cable networks, and syndicators is severely hampered by the rules, naturally leading these groups to favor the rules and the networks to oppose them.

Two general themes of this book are that regulation itself can create or reinforce interest groups and that it is possible to make predictions about which groups affected by regulation are likely or unlikely to coalesce into effective interest groups. Both these themes are illustrated by the role of interest groups in the debate over the network restrictions. They are equally well illustrated by the fate of proposals to repeal the fifty-five mile-per-hour speed limit. While repeal of this regulation has often been proposed in Congress, the issue has not attracted much support, has been strongly opposed by some, and has never progressed far enough to be voted on.

The Fifty-five Mile-per-Hour Speed Limit

The major benefits claimed for the lower speed limit are energy savings and reduced highway fatalities. The major costs imposed by the rule are increases in travel time and truck freight transportation costs. Lower speeds mean that more drivers and trucks are needed to deliver a given amount of material. A small academic literature tends to indicate that the costs of the rule outweigh the benefits.[5] Whatever the net benefits, the costs are substantial. There is, therefore, an interesting question: why have those who bear the costs of the lower limit not organized a campaign for repeal? Why have those who would be hurt by repeal been so effective in promoting their views?

To answer these questions it is necessary first to ascertain who benefits and who loses from the lower speed limit. The costs of the lower speed limit are spread widely. All consumers bear some costs, in the form of inconvenience and higher prices for final commodities because of higher transportation costs. Companies that use trucks to ship their products are also presumably hurt by the lower speed limit. Their costs are increased. But for most consumers and companies the effect will be small, since transportation costs are usually a small percentage of total costs. In any case, the cost increases apply more or less equally to all competitors in an industry and thereby significantly disadvantage only a few marginal firms.

Some individuals may feel that they benefit from the law because of the slight reduction in the chance of being involved in an accident. We do not know whether this view is generally shared by the citizenry. Many drivers routinely choose to violate the speed limit, however, and are obviously and noisily upset if their progress is delayed by a law-abiding citizen ahead of them on the highway. Such citizens presumably favor repeal of the rule at least as it applies to themselves.

But the most influential interest groups are those who have direct and perhaps substantial economic interests in the perpetuation of the lower speed limit. One strong source of organized support for the fifty-five mile-per-hour limit is the trucking industry. Trucking companies and drivers would certainly suffer economic losses if the limit were repealed, for repeal would immediately increase the productivity of the trucking industry. Each truck and driver could make more trips in a given period of time, so that fewer trucks and drivers could transport the same amount of freight. Price reductions could presumably restore full capacity utilization, but the industry might rationally fear that the net effect would be lower incomes for truckers and trucking companies. The specters of increased unemployment among truck drivers, more excess capacity among operators, and subsequent reductions in prices, wages, and profits provide each group with a strong economic interest for opposing repeal.

The interest of truck drivers and trucking company operators in the fifty-five mile-per-hour limit was actually created by the imposition of the limit. Prior to enactment the drivers and operators might have supported the lower limit because they could expect transitional gains (higher prices and wages) before new capacity was added to the industry. They might also have reasoned, prior to passage, that such gains would be transitory and would lead to higher costs. Moreover, because trucking was then subject to price regulation, truckers might expect that some time would pass before prices were allowed to rise to reflect the higher costs. All of these reasons led to neutrality or opposition to the lower limit prior to its passage. Now that the limit is in place and the industry has adjusted to it there can be no question about the economic effect of repeal on the industry. It will be hurt. This is another excellent illustration of the general point that regulation can create interests in the perpetuation of regulation even where none existed before. Thus, a rule once in place may have far stronger support than it originally commanded, even though the rule might impose greater costs than benefits on the public. A corollary of this point is that one regulatory constraint can create a constituency that clamors for further regulation. This is quite vividly illustrated by the battle taking place within the real estate services industries over repeal of section 8 of the Real Estate Settlement Practices Act of 1974, which outlaws certain payments made by title insurance companies to real estate brokers.

Rebates in Real Estate Services

President Reagan proposed in 1982 that Congress repeal section 8 of the Real Estate Settlement Practices Act of 1974, which prohibits the payment of kickbacks and rebates by title insurance companies and other providers of ancillary real estate services. The debate over this proposal has been long and heated, with many different factions within the real estate services industry.

In many states insurance regulation (together with the McCarran-Ferguson federal antitrust exemption) allows title insurance companies to fix prices. Title companies tended, however, to compete away the gains from their price fixing in payments to the real estate agents who referred business to them. Section 8 of the act makes such payments a federal crime, thus helping the title companies to maintain their price-fixing profits. If section 8 is repealed, at least some of the excess profits will be passed on to consumers as a result of competition among real estate brokers.[6]

The rules against rebates have created an interest group of title companies owned by real estate brokers that would not exist but for the rebate prohibition. In order to avoid the prohibition, brokers have opened title insurance agencies in their offices. This vertical integration allows the illegal rebates to be paid in the form of legal commissions and dividends. That they did not own such agencies before the Real Estate Settlement Practices Act suggests that brokers would prefer not to be title insurance agents. Indeed, the interest of real estate brokers in the whole subject would be minimal were it not for state insurance regulations that give rise to the excess profits and hence to the incentive to compete through rebates. Many title insurance firms have pressed for regulations or legislation that would outlaw these vertical arrangements. Thus, we find one interest group created by the system of regulation and another pressing to retain the benefits that it obtains from regulation by seeking additional regulation. Regulation itself can give rise to demands for more regulation, either by adversely affected groups or by beneficiaries of regulation who argue that the original rules did not go far enough.

The analysis of the interest groups created by state insurance regulation is relatively simple. But there are some deregulation debates in which the problem of identifying interests is complex. We turn now to the area of new drug licensing, where these analytic problems are more difficult. The debate over drug patent life extension is another example of new regulations being proposed in response to the distortions caused by old ones.

Regulatory Reform in New Drug Applications

New drugs to be marketed in the United States are subjected to a period of rigorous testing, subject to Food and Drug Administration (FDA) supervision, followed by up to two years of official government review of the test results. Consequently, the time between inventing and marketing a new drug in America can easily exceed a decade. While even drug manufacturers would not want to cut significantly the testing of new drugs, they argue that delays in the FDA approval process raise the cost of new drugs, threaten business predictability, and cause many needed drugs to be available overseas long before they are approved for use here.

Two reforms have been proposed to answer this concern. Patent extension bills in the House and Senate would extend patent life for new drugs to compensate for the delays introduced by the FDA approval process. Meanwhile, both the Carter and the Reagan administrations have undertaken extensive efforts to streamline that process. This has already resulted in an increase in the number of new drugs approved, as well as a decline in the number of enforcement actions taken by the FDA in the marketplace.[7]

An interesting feature of the debate over patent extension is that both sides claim to be placing greater reliance on market incentives. Because the FDA approval process amounts to a regulatory constraint, lengthening the patent period would permit drug companies to profit from inventions to the same extent enjoyed by firms in nonregulatory environments. The arguments of the drug companies here are analogous to those of the broadcast networks. Both would like to have an opportunity to exploit their business skills under the same rules that other companies enjoy. The pharmaceutical firms claim, moreover, that the de facto shortening of the patent period by regulatory review creates a disincentive for research in an industry where greater investment in research is in the public interest.

The interests of the pioneer pharmaceutical firms in the debate over patent life extension are fairly clear-cut. Similarly clear-cut are the interests of drug manufacturers that specialize in marketing low-priced "generic" drugs after patents have expired. They oppose extension of patent life. Both groups, of course, favor decreased delays in the FDA approval process.

The interests of drug retailers, health professionals, and consumers are decidedly more complex. In fact, both interests and views vary substantially within these groups, making them difficult to organize effectively.

Consumers, for example, have interests that vary according to their age and state of health. Older consumers with health problems have relatively little to gain from future long-term research, and more to gain from lower prices for existing drugs. They also have less to fear from harmful side effects of drugs that have long latency periods (as with most carcinogens). Younger or healthier consumers have relatively more to gain from encouraging future research. They also are more concerned about being safe from long-term carcinogens and mutagens. Similarly, drug retailers' stands on patent extension vary according to the mix of generics and brand-name pharmaceutials that each distributes. Small druggists, concerned with liability problems, tend to support the pioneer drug companies. The position of health professionals is also diverse. Different physicians and pharmacists may evaluate the trade-off between innovation and retail price competition differently. Both the AMA and the American Pharmacists' Association have nevertheless come out quietly in favor of patent extension.

Among the interest groups not represented at all in the debate are pioneer companies that would exist if the FDA delays did not reduce the economic return from new research.

Consumer advocate groups have been active in opposing patent life extension. They argue that an important interest of consumers lies in lower current drug prices. They also point out that there are other industries in which patents are not regarded as effective for the full term of a patent, such as the semiconductor and chemical industries, where greater competition has, if anything, stimulated innovation. Finally, they supported the recently enacted bill to promote research on "orphan drugs" as a more effective, targeted strategy to enhance the inventory of drugs. This program provides tax subsidies for developing new drugs to treat illnesses that are not widespread enough to provide sufficient profit incentives for drug company research.

Patent life extension is but one possible response to the problem of FDA red tape. The FDA's review of procedures for the approval of new drug applications (NDAs) and the regulatory reforms proposed by former Commissioner of Food and Drugs Donald Kennedy attack the problem more directly.

Recently both the pioneer and the generic drug manufacturers have supported steps to speed all NDA proceedings. There is a broad industry-wide consensus on reducing the number of points along the path to introduction of a drug at which regulatory review is required, and on imposing deadlines on the FDA, which, when reached without FDA action, give automatic approval to proceed to the next stage of the testing and marketing process. But some consumer groups oppose speeding up all NDA proceedings. They applaud the record of safety in America and question whether safeguards will continue to be adequate. They have, however, favored speedier processes for generics and breakthrough drugs.

The drug debate shows that there are groups whose interests are difficult to reflect in the policy debate because of their heterogeneity, because of the difficulty of identifying their members, or because of the remote stakes of each member in the outcome. In the discussion of auto emissions standards that follows, we will see another example of groups created by regulation itself, and more important, the nonrepresentation of one of the most important groups affected by the standards—automobile owners.

Automobile Emissions Standards

Reform of the standards and procedures for regulating pollution from automobiles continues to be a highly controversial area of public policy. Several issues are currently being hotly contested, encouraged in part by the debate over revisions in the nation's flagship legislation in environmental policy, the Clean Air Act.

The desirability of a uniform national emissions standard for automobiles is in dispute. Meteorological conditions, geography, altitude, and traffic densities all affect the relationship between auto emissions and air pollution from region to region. One proposal is a "two-car" strategy: to have one automobile emissions standard in regions with the most severe air pollution problems and another for the rest of the country.

The argument in favor of allowing auto emissions standards to vary from region to region is that it would save costs in areas with little or no air pollution problem. The argument against it is that it would raise the cost of enforcement. Each region that had tough emissions requirements would have to implement a system to prevent people from importing automobiles from regions with relatively lax standards.

Another controversy is whether the standard should be the same for all models or whether it should be set as a fleet-wide average. Emissions are more cheaply controlled from less powerful engines, so the total costs of achieving any given emissions ceiling would be lower if emissions reductions were made mostly from small cars.

A third issue is the appropriate balance between auto emissions controls and controls on stationary sources of pollution, such as power plants. The current practice is to divide responsibility for standards among federal, state, and local authorities according to the nature of the source. Auto emissions standards are primarily a federal responsibility, whereas the majority of standards for stationary sources are set by local authorities. This fragmented responsibility means that relatively little attention has been given to the problem of determining the most efficient division of abatement efforts between stationary and mobile sources. Several studies have argued that total abatement costs could be reduced by relaxing auto emissions standards and increasing the strictness of standards for emissions from stationary sources.[8]

Fourth, in recent years the Environmental Protection Agency has pushed state and local authorities to adopt mandatory vehicle inspection and maintenance programs. Evidence is accumulating that emissions control systems do not operate effectively over the entire 50,000-mile life that is required by current standards and guaranteed by manufacturer warranties. The primary focus of the debate is over the proper placement of responsibility for this problem: on drivers, on vehicle manufacturers, or on manufacturers of emissions control systems. Mandatory inspection and maintenance programs place primary responsibility on the automobile owner, who will have to pay for the inspection and for any repairs (other than replacement of an emissions control device that is still under warranty). The primary responsibility for designing an inspection program falls on state and local governments, much as they now are responsible for stationary source inspection programs.

For a mandatory inspection program to be within reasonable costs to motorists, inspection of the vehicles must be simple. Comprehensive vehicle inspection requires placing a vehicle in an enclosed chamber and running it over a driving cycle for a substantial period of time. Obviously, such a comprehensive approach makes sense only for a statistical sample of vehicles, not for the entire fleet. It therefore places the primary responsibility for meeting standards on automobile and emissions control manufacturers. This has implications with respect to income distribution and political acceptability as well as efficiency.

A final controversy surrounding the automobile is the promotion of alternative fuels. The two principal contenders are diesel fuel and methanol. Diesel fuels permit automobiles to use less energy per mile of operation. Historically, diesel fuel has also been somewhat cheaper than gasoline; this probably would not continue, however, if demand for diesel caused it to become the principal determinant of the output mix in oil refining. Diesel also produces a very different combination of emissions: it would generally reduce the emissions of components of photochemical smog, but would significantly increase emissions of particulate matter, a possible carcinogen.

Although it is more expensive than gasoline, methanol can be produced domestically from grains and other vegetable products. It is an especially clean fuel. Automobiles powered by methanol produce one bad pollutant—formaldehyde—which can be controlled relatively cheaply. Unfortunately, at the federal level the virtues of a methanol strategy have been debated primarily in the context of energy policy. Environmental implications have received secondary attention.

Recent debate has focused increasingly on whether the emissions ceiling for autos ought to be relaxed and whether it ought to be applied uniformly everywhere. This battle involves some major economic interests, each of which takes a predictable stand.

The automobile manufacturers support a relaxation in emissions standards that, they claim, will reduce the cost of an automobile by $300. In a normal year in which 10 million new passenger cars are sold, this amounts to a cost saving of $3 billion.[9] Automobile manufacturers obviously hope that a $300 cost reduction will yield more profits, and perhaps, if they reduce prices, more sales. Moreover, because emissions are more costly to control from large cars, they may hope to narrow the price difference between large and small cars and thereby recapture some of the market lost to foreign manufacturers.

The Manufacturers of Emissions Controls Association (MECA), a trade association representing the sellers of emissions control equipment, has lobbied vigorously to retain the current standards. Obviously, they stand to lose revenues if the automobile producers return to a simpler emissions control technology. MECA has argued that the current technology, including electronic ignition, three-way catalysts, and oxygen sensors, has contributed to improved performance and fuel economy. In congressional testimony, MECA has argued that the upper limit of cost savings from relaxation of the statutory standards would be $150 per car, not $300.

Because environmental regulation is a responsibility shared by all three levels of government, a major organized interest in the debate over automobile controls consists of regulators from state and local government. Local regulators have opposed any relaxation of automobile emissions control standards. A relaxed standard for automobile emissions would force local regulators in highly polluted areas to write more rigorous standards for stationary sources, imposing economic and political costs on state and local governments.

Environmental groups also oppose any change in automobile regulation. In part, their opposition is strategic: they prefer not to open the Clean Air Act to amendment on the fear that they have more to lose than to gain in the present political climate. In part, their opposition is based on an underlying philosophy of "technology-forcing" regulation designed to minimize emissions. They maintain that economic efficiency arguments should be given relatively little weight. Their objective is simply to make air cleaner everywhere. Relaxing a standard when it is technically possible to satisfy it is therefore certain to be opposed by environmental groups.

Within the automobile industry, the issue of averaging emissions across models, rather than having a uniform standard for all cars, is controversial. General Motors, with many model lines, is enthusiastic about the proposal. Ford argues that it deserves study. Chrysler and American Motors fear that it will disadvantage smaller, single-line companies. Economic efficiency would probably require at least some flexibility across model lines, but with Chrysler already surviving on government-guaranteed loans, any change in this direction will be scrutinized carefully by Congress.

Inspection and maintenance programs also receive considerable attention. Auto manufacturers prefer the mandatory, universal system that shares responsibility for poor performance among automobile owners, emissions control device manufacturers, and state and local governments. Another interest group has entered this debate: the people who inspect and repair vehicles. This group favors a system whereby every automobile will be inspected and owners will need to have repairs made before passing the test. Only environmentalists favor comprehensive testing. They also want to have a mandatory, uniform system to encourage proper vehicle maintenace.

Automobile owners are unrepresented in these debates. To the extent that they care about air quality, they are represented by environmental groups. To the extent that they care about the cost of new autos, they are represented by auto manufacturers. But nowhere is there systematic, comprehensive representation of their interests. Such representation would require taking account of the full costs (including the energy-related costs) of operating an automobile, as well as the proper trade-offs between automobile controls and standards for other sources. Drivers would presumably be interested in more cost-effective methods for reducing total emissions from autos, such as substituting fuel injection for carburetion and making a concomitant relaxation of tailpipe emissions controls.

None of the organized interests is concerned with policy at this level. MECA wants to enhance the tailpipe device business, whereas auto manufacturers want to reduce the costs of complying with regulation. Environmentalists want more controls at every stage, and state and local regulators are jockeying with EPA, each trying to get the other to bear as much of the political cost of developing and enforcing regulations as possible. Farmers and oil companies are squaring off over the issue of promoting methanol, but this debate has not yet spilled over into environmental policy.

Political debates about auto emissions standards have often reflected bitter divisions among the interest groups that are able to find representation in the process. But the environmental area is not the only one that has this characteristic. Energy regulation also has its private factions, as we shall see in the discussion of natural gas deregulation that follows. And like the Clean Air Act standards, which created such new interest groups as MECA, natural gas regulation has created its own interests with a stake in perpetuating the status quo.

Natural Gas Deregulation

Public regulation of natural gas markets has frequently sparked rancorous political battles. Discord in natural gas policy debates and the resulting inability of the policy process to arrive at solutions that serve the public's general interest have been the consequences of the extreme complexity and detail of natural gas regulation. The prevalence of special categories, clauses, exceptions, and exemptions has consistently split otherwise "natural" consumer, producer, and distributor interest groups into multiple factions, each with vested interests in particular components of policy. The difficulty of mediating these interests has thus far prevented policy makers from wiping the slate clean and undertaking fundamental regulatory reform.

The regulation of natural gas markets takes place at several stages. The federal government regulates selling prices charged by gas producers. Natural gas pipelines are subject to both federal and state regulation, typically of the rate-of-return variety, of their sales to retail gas utilities; and state public utility commissions regulate the operations and prices of local distribution systems. The federal role began with pipeline regulation under the Natural Gas Act of 1938 and was extended to field price setting for gas sold in interstate commerce in 1954. By the mid-1970s, these federal price controls on natural gas had produced the classic results described in economic textbooks: demand at regulated prices exceeded available supply. Consumers in interstate markets faced severe shortages. The political consequence was the Natural Gas Policy Act of 1978 (NGPA).

The central thrust of the NGPA is ostensibly some measure of deregulation of natural gas prices designed to prevent the recurrence of shortages. The act passed by Congress, however, may actually have worsened the allocation of natural gas resources.[10]

The act extended price controls to previously unregulated intrastate markets. This discouraged production but simultaneously increased the relative profitability of selling to interstate buyers. It also created an incredible array of gas categories, each of which receives a distinct price and schedule of gradual price escalation. The NGPA also removed price ceilings on gas from deep wells and, by 1985, on gas from newly developed properties. This combination of partial deregulation and the disparate effects of the NGPA's complicated provisions across interest groups have resulted in the current move toward further regulatory reform. Proposals for "reform," however, range from immediate and full decontrol to blocking further implementation of the NGPA and reimposing tight ceilings on all gas.

The NGPA has produced a number of significant and well-recognized anomalies and economic distortions.[11] The act was originally designed to allow the price of new natural gas to rise gradually to market-determined levels. Gas and oil are close substitutes, and market prices for gas are at parity with prevailing oil prices. The very sharp rise in oil prices in 1979–1980, however, left NGPA escalation rates too low. Thus, there is a strong likelihood that natural gas prices could make a sharp and politically unpalatable jump in 1985. Industrial, residential, and commercial consumers are accustomed to artificially cheap natural gas. They are thus motivated to oppose further moves toward deregulation. The magnitude of per company stakes has put utilities near the front of industrial sector opposition to decontrol, while a homogeneity of interests has brought residential and commercial consumer interest lobbies into the fray.

One of the most anomalous results of the NGPA is that, in at least some regions of the country, the price of natural gas has already been pushed to and perhaps even above free market levels. This development has taken place rapidly and has been felt as a shock by customers who have seen prices rise by as much as 50 percent over the last year.[12] The NGPA caused this because its multifarious price caps interact in curious ways with pipeline regulation.

Pipelines are regulated by setting both long-distance and local distribution rates on the basis of average costs. A pipeline purchasing gas from producers is assured that a particularly high price paid for a given portion of its overall acquisitions can be recouped by forcing up average costs. Thus, a pipeline with access to low-cost, low-ceiling-price old gas can effectively cross-subsidize its purchases of high-cost gas (for example deregulated deep gas) so long as the average-cost price ultimately charged consumers is competitive with alternative fuels. Because the total profits of a pipeline or a distribution company increase with total deliveries and because there is a shortage of low-priced gas at ceiling prices, pipelines have the economic incentive to engage in precisely such cross-subsidization.

Pipeline bidding for deregulated gas has had two general effects. First, gas supplies that are deregulated have increased in price. Deregulated gas prices at the wellhead in 1982 reached twice the level they would attain in a completely unregulated market.[13] Second, where gas prices are regulated, competition among buyers has led to contract terms favorable to producers. Most notable among these are take-or-pay provisions, which require pipelines to pay for specified quantities of gas even if the pipeline cannot take such gas because of a lack of customers. These provisions primarily affect high-cost gas supplies and have dramatically distorted the purchasing decisions of affected pipelines. The recent recession depressed demand for gas, particularly in the industrial sector, and reduced the load requirements of many pipelines. Some pipelines as a result have turned away low-cost gas rather than pay for, but give up, high-cost gas. This behavior by pipelines has been strongly criticized by customers, and the resulting high gas prices have served consumer advocates as arguments for recontrol. The behavior, however, has simply been a privately rational response to regulatory incentives.

The competition for natural gas supplies has been, and after 1985 will continue to be, unequal across pipelines. Pipelines with relatively large endowments of low-priced gas supplies have been given a "cushion" of revenues with which to cross-subsidize high-priced purchases. This cushion is based on the difference between the delivered price based on the average cost the market will bear and the cost of low-priced endowments. As a result of past regulation, pipeline cushions tend to be largest in the interstate market (that is, at the time the NGPA was signed, intrastate prices and thus ceilings were generally higher than interstate prices). The result is not only a competitive disadvantage for intrastate pipelines, but a distortion in the allocation of gas among consumers. Customers with lower-valued uses served by large-cushion pipelines are able to obtain gas while customers with higher-valued uses served by small-cushion pipelines go unsatisfied.[14] These consequences will gradually be dissipated under the NGPA as low-cost older gas supplies are used up, but it would take well into the late 1980s to accomplish this. Meanwhile, public policy will continue to lead interstate and intrastate pipelines and their respective customers to have divergent interests in natural gas debates.

Producers of natural gas gain from higher prices, and the NGPA has held the national average of producer prices below the market level. It should not be concluded, however, that producers unanimously support immediate and full deregulation. Those producers currently selling deregulated deep gas at (cross-) subsidized prices, for example, are better off under the NGPA, as would be producers of gas deregulated in 1985. The nation's economy, however, suffers from the inefficiency of regulations that induce producers to explore for and develop relatively expensive supplies while cheaper, but price-controlled, resources lie idle.

Rapidly rising natural gas prices in some markets, subsidies for some types of gas production and price ceilings on others, competitive and revenue boosts to some pipelines at the expense of others—all of these anomalies contribute to current political pressure to alter the NGPA. If the administration and Congress open the issue they will be confronted by a tangled web of interest groups. Some customer groups have coalesced because of their homogeneity and the size of the stakes and can be expected to continue to support moves toward recontrol. Pipeline companies do not benefit from the discouragement of production that price controls bring. Interstate pipelines nevertheless can generally be expected to support the type of gradual deregulation embodied in the NGPA. Intrastate pipelines, however, have an interest in more rapid decontrol. Finally, natural gas producers are well organized politically through trade associations and include some of the largest corporations in the country. They too, however, cannot act with one voice, as the NGPA has split their interests.

Conclusion

Chapter 1 has been designed to whet the reader's appetite. We have summarized half a dozen disparate regulatory areas now on the policy agenda: deregulation of network television, the fifty-five mile-per-hour speed limit, real estate settlement costs, FDA drug licensing reform, auto exhaust standards, and natural gas prices. Despite the disparity of the issues, the underlying pattern is similar. The future of regulation in these areas is being decided in an environment of interest group pressures and representation that is often entirely predictable. If it is predictable, is it possible for the policy maker and the public to assess the likely strengths and weaknesses of the arguments and the information with which they are presented? What about the groups that are not heard at all?

Chapter 2 will explore the basis in political/economic theory for making predictions about interest group motives and participation in deregulatory debates.

Notes

1. For general surveys of the literature on the economics of regulation, see Roger G. Noll and Paul L. Joskow, "Regulation in Theory and Practice: An Overview" in Gary Fromm, ed., *Studies in Public Regulation* (Cambridge, Mass.: MIT Press, 1981); Bruce M. Owen and Ronald Braeutigam, *The Regulation Game* (Cambridge, Mass.: Ballinger, 1978); Sam Peltzman, "Toward a More General Theory of Regulation," *Journal of Law and Economics*, vol. 19, no. 2 (1976), p. 211; Leonard W. Weiss and Michael W. Klass, eds., *Case Studies in Regulation* (Boston: Little, Brown, 1981).

2. Here and throughout this book the term "network" is used synonymously with ABC, CBS, and NBC, the three major national advertiser-supported commercial television broadcast networks. There are other sorts of television networks, such as the Public Broadcasting System or commercial and noncommercial satellite-distributed cable network services, but the FCC rules here in question were designed to apply only to these three companies, and as yet no others have fallen within the FCC's technical definitions. Also, network "regulation" and "deregulation" are defined for our purposes solely in terms of program supply, that is, they refer only to regulations that affect the relationship between the networks and program suppliers and syndicators. They do not include other FCC regulations such as those that affect network-affiliate relationships or political broadcasting.

3. Syndication is the licensing and distribution of feature films and television programs to local television stations on a station-by-station basis.

4. Federal Communications Commission Network Inquiry Special Staff, *New Television Networks: Entry, Jurisdiction, Ownership and Regulation* (1980).

5. For example, see Charles Lave, "Potential Energy Savings in Urban Transportation," in *Economic Impact of Energy Conservation*, U. S. House of Representatives, Subcommittee on Advanced Energy Technology and Conservation of the Committee on Science and Technology (Congressional Research Service, 1979).

6. Thomas H. Stanton and John P. Brown, FTC staff, prepared statement for *Hearings on the Real Estate Settlement Procedures Act*, U.S. House of Representatives, Subcommittee on Housing and Community Development of the Committee on Banking, Finance, and Urban Affairs (September 15, 16, 1981), pp. 75-76.

7. Linda E. Demkovich, "Critics Fear the FDA Is Going Too Far in Cutting Industry's Regulatory Load," *National Journal*, vol. 14, no. 29 (July 17, 1982), pp. 1249-52.

8. Lawrence J. White, *The Regulation of Air Pollutant Emissions from Motor Vehicles* Washington, D.C.: American Enterprise Institute, 1982), chapter 6; Robert Crandall, Theodore Keeler, and Lester Lave, "The Cost of Automobile Safety and Emissions Regulation to the Consumer: Some Preliminary Results," *American Economic Review: Papers and Proceedings*, May 1982, pp. 324-27.

9. U.S. Senate, Committee on Environment and Public Works, *Hearings: Clean Air Act Oversight, Automobile Emissions Standards*, part 4, June 23, 24, and 25, 1981; U.S. House of Representatives, Subcommittee on Health and Environment of the Committee on Energy and Commerce, *Hearings on H.R. 4400 and H.R. 2310: Mobile Source Provisions*, September-December, 1981, and January 21, 1982.

10. See U.S. Department of Energy, *A Study of Alternatives to the Natural Gas Policy Act of 1978* (1981) and Glenn C. Loury, *An Analysis of the Efficiency and Inflationary Impact of the Decontrol of Natural Gas Prices* (Washington, D.C.: Natural Gas Supply Association, 1981).

11. Milton Russell, "Natural Gas Deregulation: Overview of Policy Issues" (unpublished, Resources for the Future, 1982) provides an excellent summary of these effects of the NGPA.

12. Bureau of Labor Statistics, "Consumer Prices: Energy and Food" (monthly).

13. See Catherine Good Abbot, "Is This a Natural Gas *Market*?" (U.S. Department of Energy, Office of Policy Planning and Analysis, October 15, 1982).

14. Robert C. Means, Office of Regulatory Analysis, Federal Energy Regulatory Commission, "Analysis of the Bidding Disparity between Interstate and Intrastate Pipelines" (Natural Gas Deregulation Seminar, American Enterprise Institute, March 12, 1982) discusses the relative positions of interstate and intrastate pipelines under the NGPA.

2

The Political Economy
of Deregulation:
An Overview

This chapter examines the role, motives, and behavior of organized interest groups in regulatory proceedings. It may strike some readers as cynical to observe that interest groups have an important influence on policy making. As we shall see, however, the regulatory process was consciously designed not only to recognize the activities of interest groups but also to make positive use of the information that they provide. Policy makers must recognize the special incentives of participants in the process. The information provided by interest groups can then often enlighten public policy. Policy makers must also recognize that some points of view are not likely to be represented effectively in the process. We will return to these themes later. First, we will survey the role of interest groups in political theory.

The Role of Interest Groups in a Federal System

The American form of government is based upon rationalist, egalitarian principles. One is the primacy of individual rights over the rights of the state. Another is the principle of consent—that government powers should be derived from general agreement among the citizenry that these powers are legitimate.

The Constitution, reflecting these principles, contains several provisions that strongly affect the procedures followed by government officials in making decisions. The Constitution, for example, affirms a right of citizens to participate in government decision-making processes, limits the power of government to confiscate wealth, and establishes the foundation for challenging government decisions in the courts.

The Founding Fathers, in setting up a democratic government structured to allow extensive citizen participation in policy making, were aware of an important pitfall in this form of government: the possibility that government power could be captured by special interests. The constitutional problem as seen by the founders was to set up a process in which citizen participation was guaranteed, but in a manner that protected against powerful special interests.

In number 10 of the *Federalist Papers*, James Madison analyzed "factions," or interest groups, and their potentially harmful influence in a nonfederal system of government:[1]

> By a faction I understand a number of citizens, whether amounting to a majority or a minority of the whole, who are united and actuated by some common impulse of passion, or of interest, adverse to the rights of other citizens, or to the permanent and aggregate interests of the community.

Madison and his colleagues sought to design a system of government that would be able not merely to resist the harmful effects of "factions" but to harness their energy to the common good:

> The regulation of those various and interfering interests forms the principal task of modern legislation and involves the spirit of party and faction in the necessary and ordinary operations of government.

The idea was simple: create a federal representative government in which each faction or interest was represented but had relatively little power. That government, properly designed, could balance the various special interests, while providing adequate opportunities for each to persuade a majority of the merits of its position. No one faction could succeed in tyrannizing the rest.

A similar set of concerns underlies the design of the regulatory policy process. Policy is made in the context of organized persuasive activity by competing interest groups with something to gain or lose from the outcome. These interest groups are often composed of industries, industry segments, individual firms, and labor organizations. Consumers and the general public are not as well represented. Even consumer groups or public interest groups often have interests that, though allied with consumers' interests, may differ in important ways, as Robert Crandall's case study of environmental regulation vividly illustrates (chapter 5).

Interest groups provide regulators with information, analysis, and argument that, properly used, can serve the interest of the general citizenry. Much of the information and analysis would be difficult or impossible for policy makers or their staffs to compile independently. Interest groups hire able advocates and analysts whose work would otherwise have to be done by the same staffs that help the decision makers evaluate the arguments. When competing interest groups are forced to provide the decision makers with costly data, analysis, and argument, the policy decision is likely to be a better one, provided that the decision makers recognize and take account of the biases that result from the special advantage or disadvantage that each group expects from the proposed action.

Each group naturally takes positions and makes arguments that it regards as economically beneficial to itself. The regulator's job is to sift these arguments, to identify those that arise from self-interest and are concerned only with self-interest, and to discover valid arguments that arise from self-interest but are concerned also with the interest of consumers. Regulators must also recognize that some legitimate interests may not be represented in the debate—perhaps because regulation has prevented their formation.

The constitutional principles of broad representation, rights of participation, protection of private property, and due process have all had major effects on the way the regulatory agencies make decisions. The agencies are usually very specialized, dealing with a sharply focused set of policy issues that are rarely of widespread political salience. Moreover, they affect the distribution of wealth in society not by direct expenditures of funds but by creating the ground rules by which the economy operates. This makes them an unimportant part of the budgetary process, easily overlooked in the range of government activities even if their impact is great. For these reasons, they are especially vulnerable to becoming obscure and are therefore subject to excessive special interest influence.

One form of protection against this outcome is the formal procedure by which agencies reach decisions. The constitutional principles discussed above have been interpreted by the courts and codified as procedural rules for agency decisions. These include quasi-judicial rules regarding evidence and participation in processes and the requirement that agency decisions be based upon information and analysis acquired through a relatively open process. Agencies must show that their decisions respond reasonably to a statutory mandate, recognize the evidence presented to them, and have a substantial basis in the records of the proceeding that led to them. Moreover, people disaffected with an agency's decision have the right to appeal it to the federal court system for failure to adhere to these standards.

These rules have two somewhat opposing effects. First, because the process is formal and legalistic, it is expensive for participants, which militates against broad representation in the process. Second, it protects against a special interest orientation by the agencies because it requires them to pay attention to all who are represented. One key to the performance of this process, then, is whether the first effect is sufficiently weak that broad participation nonetheless emerges.

The Forms of Economic Interests

Networks, Hollywood studios, viewers, and other groups each have economic interest in the outcome of the debate on network deregulation. The same is true for drivers, truckers, and ordinary citizens in the case of the fifty-five mile-per-hour speed limit. In these cases, as in regulatory contexts generally, the economic interest of a group in a debate over regulatory policy can take several forms. The most straightforward example, and the most widely analyzed and recognized, is when an industry uses regulation to establish a form of cartel that is to some extent insulated from attack on antitrust grounds. Because true cartels are relatively easy to detect and politically very vulnerable, regulation rarely produces such a result for very long. A more modest, more attainable objective is for a group to seek some special advantages that it could not obtain under the disciplines of normal market processes.

Among producer groups, common examples are rules that establish cost-based minimum prices to buttress profits during periods of slack business, government assistance in averting competitive risk (for example, loan guarantees), and entry barriers that protect incumbent firms. All regulatory agencies have had experience with this phenomenon. The FCC's regulations restricting the importation of distant television signals by cable systems—including a total freeze during an extended period in the late 1960s and early 1970s—created important actual or perceived benefits to local broadcast stations by limiting competition from cable television services.[2] The rules were originally motivated by a desire to protect viewers' interest in local programming. But groups of local stations that benefited had an interest in opposing deregulation and advocated that the restrictions be retained. The commission eventually found, however, that the regulations were not beneficial to consumers.

Suppliers of goods and services to an industry normally have a stake in its regulation. Suppliers can be expected to oppose a cartel in the regulated industry because cartels restrict output and thereby reduce the regulated industry's demand for inputs. But suppliers, such as industry-wide unions, may take the opposite point of view if they have monopoly power over the regulated industry; then the gains derived from regulation by the cartel can be extracted by the monopolistic supplier.

Suppliers may also have reason to favor regulation in a competitive industry that succeeds in setting prices above the competitive level, but that does not control other forms of competition. Regulated firms can then be expected to compete by improving product quality, which may require even greater use of some inputs than would price competition.

Examples of suppliers taking positions with these motivations abound in the transportation sector. The Teamsters union strongly advocates trucking regulation, and rail workers unions tend to favor regulation of the railroads. These unions have been especially adept at capturing a share of the excess profits derived from the anticompetitive effects of regulation, either through very effective wage bargaining or through featherbedding. In the case of airlines, airline pilots opposed deregulation on the ground that competition would erode safety. But research on the airlines demonstrates that airline regulation created competition in flight-schedule frequency—for example, by causing airlines to fly a greater number of flights with fewer passengers per flight. Pilots feared that deregulation would reduce the airlines' demand for pilots.

In contrast to the pilots, aircraft manufacturers were largely neutral on airline deregulation, although early in the debate they expressed concern about the effects of deregulation on purchases of new aircraft. Whatever their private preferences and expectations, as the debate proceeded they remained officially neutral, not wishing to offend their airline customers, who were badly split on the issue.

Opportunity arises for user groups as well as supplier groups to seek advantage through the regulatory process. In regulated industries supply shortages are normally dealt with by administrative rules regarding user priorities, rather than by letting prices increase until the market clears. User groups seek to attain for themselves higher priority than that enjoyed by others. During the oil supply shortages of 1973 and 1979, for example, agricultural interests were especially effective in receiving fuel supply allocations at essentially no reduction from previous free market levels.

Regulation also creates opportunities for user groups to seek special breaks in the price structure of regulated firms. In nearly all regulated industries, firms provide a variety of products or services, some of which are supplied to a particular, identifiable industry or other organized group. Such a group has an interest in making sure that the prices it is charged are as low as possible. Because regulated prices tend to be based upon costs, the debate is often over costing principles. Regulators are forced to undertake a process that sellers would otherwise undertake for themselves in response to the market, namely to allocate among various products or services the common costs of the business. Each user group can be expected to advocate a costing principle that allows the service it uses to be priced favorably.

Both suppliers and users have stakes in decisions by regulators about the nature of the regulated product. While regulated firms provide a variety of services, the economics of production will normally preclude the possibility of tailoring services to suit exactly the most desired characteristics of every user. Regulation provides a forum in which the characteristics of the service can be debated, whether it be the number of hours of community service or locally produced broadcasting, or the number of ounces of meat in an airline meal. These regulations determine which customers will be best served by the particular configuration of attributes in a regulated product and which suppliers will be most helped by these constraints.

Users and suppliers alike, as well as regulated businesses, also have a stake in how regulatory rules allocate business risks. Businesses must make long-term capital investments based on only partly predictable economic variables such as customer tastes, the state of the economy, the possibility of product and process innovation, and the prices of inputs and competing products. Regulatory rules decide not only how suppliers, users, and regulated firms will fare if things work out as expected but also how they will bear the risks and rewards of unanticipated events.

In an unregulated world, two common means of coping with risk are risk-pooling contracts and vertical integration. Both provide a buyer and a seller a means to guarantee stability in a business relationship, either by agreeing to the terms of a continuing flow of transactions long in advance or by merging the two activities.

In a regulated environment, whether a firm can use these strategies, and if so in what form, are matters for regulators to decide. The reason is justifiable: without regulatory scrutiny in some situations regulated firms can use long-term contracts and vertical integration to preclude regulators from attaining their policy objectives. Such arrangements can lock in a particular pattern of business decisions and prices that regulators might wish to change in the future. They can also help a regulated firm escape a constraint on the overall rate of return of one part of the business.

An additional feature of risk-spreading arrangements, however, is that companies that are not party to them generally must assume greater risk. These arrangements do not remove the risk from an industry; instead businesses agree to share with their suppliers and/or customers the brunt of an unexpected event. Obviously, these other groups would like to prevent this from happening, and if possible to obtain regulatory rulings that transfer the burden of risk to still others.

Regulation as an Element of Corporate Planning

Each of the parties to the debate on network deregulation must anticipate possible shifts in regulatory policy in planning its future. The same is true for the drug companies whose marketing activities are regulated by the FDA, for the title insurance companies regulated by state insurance commissioners, and for most regulated industries. Indeed, some firms may prefer to avoid deregulation simply because they have learned to operate well under the regulatory process as part of their overall corporate plans.

The regulatory process is fully capable of conferring rewards and benefits on persuasive and effective interest groups. Firms must recognize this in their planning and in their development of an overall business strategy. Indeed, a firm that discovers a way to benefit from regulation can come to have a tremendous economic stake in perpetuating a regulatory mechanism. Firms orienting their planning to take advantage of regulation will have a different mix of revenue sources, investment projects, and so on than firms that do not take strategic account of regulation. Deregulation would leave such firms in a potentially embarrassing competitive position.

The airline industry provides examples of firms that had learned to prosper under the CAB's route-awarding and fare-setting regulatory process. Such firms had a particularly difficult time coping with the competitive pressures of a deregulated market. Similarly, many trucking concerns used the ICC's anticompetitive certification process (which placed the burden of proof on the new entrant to show the economic necessity of certification) as part of their corporate strategic plans. The ICC mechanism tended to protect the certificated routes from competitive attack, leading to a different pattern of route-system development than would have occurred in a free market.

Deregulation poses a threat to another kind of firm or group: those who simply prefer the regulation game to the competition game because they happen to be better at the former. A firm that has special attributes valuable in regulated environments—advocacy skills or political connections, for example—will tend to capture larger market shares and higher profits under regulation than under a full competitive market. Such firms will constitute a particularly effective interest group opposing deregulation, even though the groups would not exist but for regulation. Other firms may simply be familiar and comfortable with life in a regulated world. Pan American, for example, was the "chosen instrument" or U.S. flag carrier in international commercial aviation, having a status much like the nationalized carriers of other countries. It was subjected to only very limited competition from other American carriers, and among the international companies operated under the protective umbrella of IATA, the cartel of international airlines. Such firms—and even their customers—may regard a movement away from the quiet life of regulation as unduly or unnecessarily risky, even if there are tangible benefits to be expected from deregulation.

Even regulation that is neutral in its effects on consumers and the competitive vigor of an industry is likely to produce a different distribution of economic benefits among the firms than would exist in a free market environment. Firms that are doing well under regulation have something to lose—their market position—and are much more likely to constitute a well-financed and organized group opposing deregulation than members of the industry at the bottom of the heap. In the debates about airline deregulation, for example, the major passenger carriers commanded the most attention, and most, such as American, Eastern, Delta, and TWA, opposed deregulation. United, the largest domestic carrier, initially opposed it but switched positions when it perceived itself to be in a strong growth position compared with other carriers and unlikely to be awarded new routes under regulation. Many small, vigorous airlines that came to flourish under deregulation—such as New York Air, Midway, and People Express—had less of a voice in the debates, though two of them—PSA and Southwest— were major participants because they had succeeded in the two largest deregulated intrastate markets, California and Texas.

Regulation as a Creator and Destroyer of Interests

The policy analysis of any proposal to repeal a rule or to deregulate must obviously take into account the self-interest of those presenting information and arguments. It may not be so obvious to consider the possibility that some interest groups may actually have been created— and others destroyed—by enactment of the rule being debated. Some interest groups may not be participating in the debate because regulation has caused them to disappear; other groups may be participating who have an interest or even existence that is artificial because it was created by the very regulations in question.

Not all the interest groups that participate in a regulatory debate would exist in the absence of the rules whose repeal is proposed. Moreover, agencies will not hear from some interests because regulatory rules have the effect of destroying the basis on which the interests could be organized, or because the groups are officially neutral and therefore silent. Chapter 1 provides several examples of the phenomenon of regulation-created interests: the industry trade group that manufactures auto emission controls, the brokers that benefit from price regulation in title insurance, the various groups with interests in continued price regulation of natural gas.

Regulations that have any effect at all—good or bad—necessarily cause the structure of the economy to depart from its unregulated state. Some firms have more business, while others have less. Some firms and products do not exist that otherwise would; other firms and products exist that would not in a free market environment. Regulation has this effect regardless of whether its net effect is beneficial to consumers. Indeed, regulation sometimes has the effect of transferring wealth from one group of consumers to another, just as it can redistribute profits from one group of firms to another. When these effects can be anticipated, they motivate participation in the debate over regulatory policy by the potential gainers and losers.

Often these effects are either intended by policy makers or reluctantly accepted as a necessary cost of achieving a desired policy objective. But effects can also be unanticipated and inadvertent. Some groups may receive unintended benefits and thereby have a vested interest in perpetuating the regulation. Indeed, it may be an inadvertent regulatory benefit that defines an interest group.

The effect of this phenomenon is that a regulation can be more strongly advocated once it is in effect than it ever was when it was being considered. Initially, the source of participation will be the *anticipated* effects on the groups that are organized to participate in the debate. When regulation is in effect, the losers will have been weakened and some will have disappeared. Meanwhile, interests created by unanticipated side effects will advocate continuation of the regulation, although they did not participate initially. Consequently, the effort required by an agency to overturn an outdated or mistaken regulation can turn out to be far greater than the effort required to establish it in the first place. This is so because outside interests are motivated to provide more evidence and analysis in support of a regulation conferring actual benefits than in support of a proposal conferring only anticipated economic benefits. This phenomenon increases the responsibility of the regulator to ensure a balanced range of inputs to the evaluation of a deregulation proposal.

Consider, for example, the case of SEC-sanctioned self-regulation of the New York Stock Exchange that before 1975 allowed the members of the exchange to fix the level of brokers' commissions.[3] The effect of this regulation was to prevent price competition and to set a uniformly high price for stock brokerage service. It also encouraged competition in services and image-oriented advertising.

Large institutional traders, whose business was especially profitable to brokers at the fixed prices, constituted a special interest group with an incentive to oppose regulation initially and to advocate deregulation because they and their customers (for example, pensioners) would tend to benefit the most from market-clearing prices. Stockbrokers favored regulation initially and opposed deregulation: the regulation made them better off by enabling them to act as a cartel to enrich themselves at the immediate expense of volume purchasers such as mutual and pension funds. By keeping prices above the competitive level, regulation not only made some brokerage firms especially profitable but also allowed some inefficient and badly managed firms to succeed. Prior to regulation, no interest group of inefficient firms existed. But regulation created such an interest, one that subsequently fought hard against deregulation.

Banks provide another illustration of how an interest group has been created by regulation. As Andrew Carron explains in his case study (chapter 4), the Federal Reserve Board's "Regulation Q" has the effect of keeping interest rates paid to small savers on passbook accounts at artificially low levels. Meanwhile, to the extent that interest rate regulation reduces interest paid on savings below competitive levels, banks can lend out the funds at interest rates above the regulated level, pocketing the difference between the two rates. The result is that an advantaged group of financial institutions is created with an interest in opposing deregulation. The losers are small savers and unsophisticated consumers.

Like banks, savings and loan institutions have been required by regulation to pay below-market rates of interest on passbook accounts. But unlike banks, savings and loan institutions are restricted in their lending activities because they are required to place most of their assets into mortgage loans. Some believe that competition among S&Ls for a limited market may force them to pass on part of their lower costs from passbook accounts in lower mortgage rates benefiting the housing industry, though as Carron points out there seems to be little evidence that this is so. In any event, there was a time when S&Ls were the only source of long-term home mortgage financing. For this reason, whether rational or not, the construction and housing industries have come to believe that they have a stake in preserving regulatory restrictions on S&Ls. The depression-era policy makers who initiated the regulations surely did not fully anticipate the new suburban bedroom communities and housing-related employment that would be created. Yet such regulations inadvertently created gainers who are now part of the resistance to deregulation.

Consider, as another example, the small refiner bias in petroleum regulation, as discussed in the case study by Joseph Kalt (chapter 6). During the period of extensive regulation of prices and allocations of crude oil and petroleum products, small refiners were given greater access to relatively cheap domestic crude and were subjected to less restrictive controls on refinery products. This encouraged the survival and entry of inefficient small refineries that otherwise would have been unable to compete with large refineries. The effect of the small refiner bias was to create a powerful interest group that derived important benefits from perpetuating petroleum regulation, without regard to the effect on the nation's energy supply problems.

As Professor Alfred Kahn points out in his case study (chapter 8), the airline industry before deregulation is still another example of an interest group created by regulation itself. Carriers with profitable routes from which entry by competitors was barred by regulation had an incentive to oppose deregulation. So did smaller communities that came to believe—for the most part, incorrectly—that regulation caused airlines to provide service to them.

Airline regulation undoubtedly produced a *different* route structure than did deregulation, because factors other than economic efficiency were used to decide which firms could serve which routes. In principle, deregulation could have immediately caused many routes to be abandoned. This would have taken place had regulation created some extremely profitable routes by severely controlling not only the number of airlines allowed to serve them but also the number of flights that each could offer, and by allowing the favored few to charge monopoly prices. Deregulation would then have caused the excluded lines to flock to these routes by switching planes from other, less profitable ones. In fact, this was not the case. Regulators never did require airlines to continue to serve routes that lost money; even had there been an initial reallocation of planes away from small towns, other carriers or commuters would have instituted service. The fears of small communities that they would lose all air service were thus not well founded.

In the airline case, the existence of formal route awards may have created the illusion that it was regulation that made service possible. Or small communities may have perceived, correctly, that they had little to gain from deregulation. The airlines serving them did not appear to be making excessive profits or giving them excessive service, so any small chance of losing service was not worth the risk. As Alfred Kahn points out, however, the overall effect of deregulation was clearly beneficial; it led to greater efficiency, lower fares, and better service for most passengers.

Resistance to Changed Circumstances

Most regulatory agencies were established during the depression in the 1930s or even earlier. The conditions and perceptions that led to regulation are no longer relevant. There is no longer an energy crisis giving rise to a rationale for the fifty-five mile-per-hour speed limit. Technology has changed in some industries. Clean air goals are perhaps not best served by the old auto emission standards. In other cases the structure of the industry is no longer the same. In the television industry, for example, FCC actions to permit the growth of cable television and pay-TV, to allow direct satellite broadcasting, and to allocate the UHF band to television have gradually eroded the market power of networks, thereby weakening the case for restraining them. Experience since the 1930s has taught us that, whatever the theoretical merits, serious inefficiencies are often the practical result of regulation. In some cases, such as trucking, direct comparison with unregulated markets has even allowed us to measure the social costs of regulation. Yet proponents of regulation often ignore or discount these changes.

One of the costs of regulation is that it creates a process that can be used to resist economic change. Regulation must be invoked to approve changes in the nature of regulated services or the way in which they are offered, and consequently retards the process by which a regulated industry responds to changes in its economic and technical environment. The presence of regulation therefore confers benefits on those who have an incentive to resist economic change. Indeed, one type of interest group created by regulation is composed of firms and industries that have become obsolete, or that benefit from obsolete services. Their primary strategy against deregulation is to obscure the fact that the market judgment about them has turned negative.

An example of this can be found in some of the opposition to railroad deregulation. The initial impetus for regulation was from some railroads, who wanted to restrict competition on routes between major cities, and some rural interests and small communities, who wanted to put an end to monopoly pricing for short-haul traffic. As the costs and demand for rail service changed, however, two kinds of service became unprofitable at any price: passenger service (principally serving the same big cities that in an earlier era had benefited from competition and opposed railroad regulation) and routes serving predominantly manufacturing shippers on small community sidings. Railroads, facing severe financial problems, sought to abandon these services.

In an unregulated industry, changes in the economic environment cause changes in prices and services. Customers respond to new and more convenient (or economical) opportunities by altering their consumption patterns. But in the world of ICC railroad regulation, abandonment of services required regulatory approval. The communities or customer groups that received unprofitable service had an interest in continued regulation. Moreover, regulation had given them rights they would not enjoy as buyers in an ordinary market: the right to continue to receive a subsidized service and to require someone else to pay, in part, for services they consumed. They retained this right until a formal regulatory decision could be made and upheld that it ought to come to an end. By creating a right to be served unless defeated in a political/legal contest, regulation led to creation of an interest group favoring preservation of its historical status in the face of changing economic circumstances that questioned the very wisdom of regulation.

Microwave and satellite technology transformed the economics of intercity telecommunications, making competition viable where it was not before. The telephone industry fought hard to preserve the regulated monopoly that was created when other technology was dominant. As a result entry and competition for intercity services were retarded.[4] It was twenty years or more before the opposition of the entrenched industry could be overcome.

Regulation of the programming and commercial practices of radio stations had been based on the notion that private interests should not determine what the public hears from a few sources. Since the FCC was created, however, the number of radio stations has grown from a few hundred to nearly 9,000. Competition for listeners among the large number of radio stations is extensive, serving to limit excessive commercialization and providing diversified programming responsive to listeners' demands. By the 1970s the FCC's radio regulation was thus no longer needed because competition had become more effective than regulation. Yet proponents of regulation, mainly political and activist groups whose interests were served by forcing radio stations to air their messages, ignored the structural changes in the market and the degree to which the regulations were anachronistic and ineffective.

Finally, there is a striking parallel between the failure of the housing industry to accept the changed circumstances that perhaps once, but no longer, justified restrictions on S&L loan portfolios and the failure to accept changed circumstances in the network program industry. Whatever the effects of the financial interest and syndication rules, the alleged problem that gave rise to them was more apparent in 1970 than in 1982, just as the need for a spur to home mortgage loans was more apparent in 1933 than in 1973.

Strategic Use of Regulation

A desire to use the regulatory process to handicap one's competitors is common. One dramatic example is the current apparent attempt by large ocean freight customers to use shippers' conferences as a device to disadvantage their smaller competitors. Incumbent firms can use the regulatory process to gain a competitive advantage over actual and potential competitors. In a number of regulated industries, competitors who desire to enter the indsutry, expand their geographic scope, or lower their prices can be opposed in regulatory proceedings. Regulated firms can use the regulatory mechanism itself to impose costs and delays on their would-be competitors, thereby deterring entry and restricting competitive responses to noncompetitive conditions.

In television markets, another good example, the networks are but one of several distribution channels. Programs are distributed also to stations as first-run or off-network properties, and first-run syndicators that use satellite distribution look increasingly like networks. In the case of creative products such as movies, distribution stages include pay-TV, networks, theaters, and cassettes or discs as well as over-the-air broadcasts. Management and coordination of the distribution of creative properties through these stages is a function in which television networks, Hollywood distributors, and others compete with each other. One effect of the FCC's financial interest and syndication rules is that the networks are largely restrained from participating in this process. This reduction in the number of competitors, if it benefits anyone, benefits the remaining firms—Hollywood studios and major syndicators.

A number of industries exclude or delay competitors by effectively using entry barriers. The telecommunications industry has witnessed lengthy proceedings to determine whether competition would be permitted. The telephone industry, especially AT&T, vigorously opposed competition. The airline and trucking industries are also examples in which incumbent firms have participated actively in the regulatory process to limit competition. Entry proposals have been opposed by incumbents, and existing firms have usually favored rules that make it more difficult for new firms to obtain approval from regulators. Similarly, price reductions have been effectively challenged in both industries by competing firms, thereby raising the costs and reducing the profitability of trying to engage in price competition.

Using the standard-setting process to competitive advantage is another regulatory strategy available to firms in some regulated industries. Setting environmental standards is one example in which the regulatory process can be manipulated, as Robert Crandall demonstrates in chapter 5. In 1977, for instance, Congress passed legislation establishing standards to control emissions of sulfur oxides from new electric generation facilities. After much debate, the rule finally established by EPA required stack-gas scrubbers of a given technical efficiency regarding the fraction of sulfur oxides removed from stack gases. This meant that the same *percentage* reduction in sulfur emissions had to be achieved no matter what the initial sulfur content of the coal was.

Coal can, however, differ dramatically in sulfur content, with western coal having especially low amounts of sulfur. For many regions, therefore, the most cost-effective approach to clean air is to burn low-sulfur coal from the West and spend relatively little on cleaning the stack gas.

Obviously, this fact did not please eastern coal interests, who lobbied successfully for standards that called for a straight percentage reduction of even the smallest amounts of sulfur. All new plants would need the same scrubbing equipment. The result was to reduce the incentive for utilities to pay the higher transportation costs to acquire western coal. An unfortunate side effect was to worsen air quality, because scrubbed gases from the burning of eastern coal are dirtier. Moreover, because the high-performance scrubbers required by the EPA are very expensive, the regulation created an added incentive to use older, dirtier, and less efficient plants not needing to meet the standards. And scrubbers in practice frequently fail, further worsening air quality.

A better approach would have been to set an absolute standard for air quality, giving the power plants some latitude in how to achieve it. But because eastern coal mining is fully developed and located in relatively populous states, while western coal is a largely undeveloped resource located in states with very low population, the eastern coal interests had the political clout to succeed in getting the standard they wanted.

Attempts have been made to use safety standards for similar anticompetitive purposes. The American bicycle industry proposed safety standards for bicycles before the Consumer Product Safety Commission (CPSC).[5] The proposed standards involved design features that effectively would have excluded foreign bicycle manufacturers. Unaware of these features, the CPSC adopted the standards. An uproar from bicyclists made the CPSC aware of the problem, and the standards were rescinded.

Consider, finally, Andrew Carron's description in chapter 4 of the securities industry's attempt to retain regulation that prevents banks from competing to underwrite municipal bonds. This is a striking case of an industry group seeking by regulation to prevent a potentially more efficient group of competitors from entering the market. It is instructive to note that in neither the securities case nor the network program case do the parties seem to be seeking to allocate rents. The fight is over the stability of markets and market shares.

Factors Affecting Successful Representation

Effective advocacy, whether in the political process, in the courts, or before a regulatory commission, costs money, often a fairly substantial amount. Indeed, the very procedures that implement constitutional principles guarding against factionalism can make it expensive to be heard, and some points of view may not be adequately expressed. It is possible to make some general statements about the kinds of groups that are likely to be well represented.

Self-Interest. The first observation to be made about participation in the regulatory process is that a participant must have an important reason to become involved. Almost always this interest is personal: the decision is perceived to have an important effect on the participant's welfare. Usually the interest is even narrower: the welfare at stake is the participant's economic position, and the interest of the participant is to receive a favorable decision about prices, service quality, or rights in the regulated market. Truly disinterested participation to advocate a general public good, while not unheard of, is extremely rare. The number of significant political and legal processes is large, and effective participation requires money and time. Consequently, most people will elect to participate only in processes in which their direct, personal stake is high. The dilemma of the regulator, not unlike the dilemma of the political representative or the jurist, is to identify the public interest amid a chorus of self-seeking arguments.

Group Size. Even among self-interested groups, not all will be equally well organized and represented. A second important factor explaining participation in the regulatory process is that, other things equal, groups with a small number of members will tend to be better able to organize and express their views than groups with many members. A group that successfully obtains a regulation or rule beneficial to its members normally will not be able to limit the benefits flowing from the regulation only to members who contributed financially to the advocacy effort. This gives members of the group an incentive not to contribute to the advocacy fund: each can expect to "free ride" by obtaining the benefits of successful advocacy without having to bear any of the costs.[6] In large groups, the incentive is especially strong because no single member will perceive that it has an important influence on the total effectiveness of the group. But to the extent a significant fraction of a group's members tries to free ride, the ability of the group to finance its advocacy efforts adequately will be severely hampered.

Groups with few members are usually better able to overcome the free rider problem. The smaller the number of members, the greater is each member's share in the benefits realized by the group. Because of this greater stake in successful advocacy, individual members of small groups are more likely to perceive that the chance of group success depends on their own individual efforts. Moreover, smaller groups can monitor more easily the contributions of each member. Groups with relatively few members are thus in a better position to apply peer pressure to members who do not contribute their fair share to the effort. This characteristic will tend to make oligopolies and monopolies more effectively organized than competitive industries, and the latter better organized than their customers.

The principle is illustrated by the extensive lobbying and political activities of the steel industry in pursuing restrictive trade policies. Because it has historically been an oligopoly, the steel industry has not faced a serious free rider problem. A dozen or so firms capture nearly all of any benefits that protectionist legislation provides for the industry. Steel customers, because they are less concentrated, are harder to organize, though one group, auto manufacturers, could surely be an effective force for free trade in steel if it did not have its own problem of coping with foreign competition.

The free rider problem is not insuperable. It merely implies, other things equal, that it is an advantage to have fewer members in an interest group. Of course, other things are not always equal, and interest groups with many members are sometimes very successful in advancing their members' interests. The analysis thus far has assumed that individual members of the interest group voluntarily contribute to an advocacy effort. Some interest groups with many members are successful because they are able to compel contributions from their members or because the group has already been effectively organized for another purpose. The Teamsters union and the maritime unions, for example, have been prominent opponents of deregulating the trucking and ocean-shipping industries, respectively. Both unions have many members, but union dues are not voluntary contributions, so the unions do not face a free rider problem in obtaining funds for advocacy. Another example is the American Automobile Association. Many of its members join because of the services it offers: roadside repairs, free maps, and the like. Yet the organization actively lobbies to advance what it perceives to be the interests of motorists.

The relationship between the size of an interest group and its chances of succeeding in obtaining regulation favorable to its members is also affected by the size and strength of the opposition. The relative, not absolute, abilities of competing groups to organize their efforts are an important element in determining the effect of interest groups. This is perhaps best illustrated by the success of competitive industries composed of many firms in retaining beneficial laws, rules, and regulations. The successful lobbying efforts of the trade associations of such industries are explained partly by the fact that their opponents are often taxpayers and consumers, who are much more numerous and face even greater free rider problems than the producers. Trucker support for the fifty-five mile-per-hour speed limit is a good example. Farming and ocean shipping are also examples of structurally competitive industries which have successfully retained not only federal subsidies but anticompetitive legislation and regulation which benefit industry members at the expense of less well-represented taxpayers and consumers.

The success of agricultural interests in obtaining favorable legislation and regulation illustrates another way in which the effects of the free rider problem have been overcome. The system of political representation devised by the Founding Fathers to protect against factionalism actually promotes it in one way because it discriminates in favor of sparsely populated states. South Dakota has the same number of senators as New York. As a result, interests that are relatively concentrated in sparsely populated states are significantly overrepresented politically. Because there is a negative correlation between the population of a state and the relative importance of its agricultural economy, it is not surprising that farm interests are clearly heard, especially in the Senate. The substantial attention that federal regulators typically devote to prices and service in sparsely populated areas is in part a response to the same political reality.

Size of the Stakes. Another factor that can attenuate the effectivenes of groups with a large number of potential beneficiaries is the absolute size of each member's interest in the outcome. If each member of a group stands to gain only a small benefit, the chances are that a successful lobbying effort cannot be organized. If, however, the absolute stakes are very large to each member, advocacy is more easily funded, even in the face of large numbers. The lobbying efforts of the maritime industry can be explained partly by the fact that the continuation of government subsidies is probably crucial to the very survival of many firms in the domestic industry.

One measure of the ability of a group to become organized for effective political participation is the degree of homogeneity of interest among the group members. Groups in which the primary objective of each member is essentially the same and can be simply stated, and in which each of the members has a similar stake in the outcome, will be easier to organize and more effective. Homogeneous groups need not spend a great deal of time ironing out differences and finding a mutually acceptable statement of purpose and need not fear defection of members who do not get what they want. In the political sphere, this characteristic is exhibited by single-issue groups that effectively oppose gun control, abortion, and evolutionary theory, even though all three of these issues are supported by a majority of the population; this characteristic is exhibited as well by the lack of success in forming an effective group for tax reform, an issue of almost universal interest but too complex and too heterogeneous to be an effective focus of political organization.

In the regulatory sphere, this phenomenon tends to favor producer groups at the expense of consumer groups. Labor organizations and trade associations largely agree that restrictions on competition among themselves enhance their economic interest. Consumers, by contrast, have widely varying stakes in decisions about price and service quality in any particular industry. If organized at all, buyers normally are fragmented into groups with relatively homogeneous interests and may orient their participation as much toward gaining advantage over other customer groups as over the regulated producer group.

Some organizations, such as "public interest" law firms or consumer organizations, regard themselves as representing the interests of all or most consumers in regulatory processes. But often they do so imperfectly at best because of two major problems. First, these groups must worry about their own survival. The regulatory process provides them with a source of power not otherwise possessed to affect market performance and, to the extent regulators consider their views, to obtain leverage over other groups. Public interest groups can be an instrument for intervening in government processes on behalf of otherwise unrepresented groups; hence they can be expected to be biased in favor of regulatory solutions and against market solutions, because their influence will be greater under a regulatory regime. Consumers who believe in such solutions will find themselves well represented by public interest groups; consumers who believe, however, that they would be better served by less regulation are not likely to be as well represented.

A second problem confronting public interest groups is the relationship they have with their constituency or client group. Consumerism is primarily a middle-class movement. Even among consumer activists, tastes in products and opinions about policy priorities are diverse. Consequently, public interest groups cannot be expected to represent all types of consumers nor to participate in a wide range of regulatory issues where consumer interests are heterogeneous.

Uncertainty. Another factor that tends to inhibit the formation of successful interest groups is uncertainty. If the effects of a regulation, or the precise identity of the beneficiaries and the losers, cannot be predicted beforehand with reasonable accuracy, the incentive to contribute to a lobbying effort is obviously reduced.

In many circumstances uncertainty will be greater about some effects of regulation than about others. If benefits are uncertain but costs are known, advocates of the status quo ante will be better represented. In environmental regulation, for example, firms may know very well what different antipollution policies will cost them, but victims of pollution may be considerably less certain of the benefits to themselves of reducing a particular pollutant from a particular source.

On the other hand, a change in rules may create new interest groups. Once the change has occurred, the uncertainty about who will benefit from the change is resolved. The large number of potential beneficiaries is transformed into what may be a considerably smaller number of actual beneficiaries. So the change in rules may result in the formation of viable interest groups by eliminating substantial impediments to their creation.

Since regulators necessarily rely on the range of views expressed by active interest groups in formulating policy, it is important to understand the forces that can produce distortion, bias, and under- or overrepresentation in that range. Large numbers, the free rider problem, heterogeneity, uncertainty, and unidentifiable interests are all likely to result in some viewpoints going unexpressed. Those who would benefit from the adoption of a particular viewpoint may not constitute a viable interest group because the interest itself is too diffuse, ill-defined, or uncertain. The interest group whose views are not heard may even be a group of businesses. Suppose, for example, that deregulation would generate market opportunities for some among a large number of potential competitors. Before deregulation, these individual firms may not be able to organize effectively. The entrants who will ultimately be successful do not yet know who they are because there is uncertainty about which firms will benefit from the change. Compound this with a large number of potential competitors, and each firm is likely to see little reason to undertake the cost and risk of contributing to an advocacy campaign.

Applications to Deregulation Debates

This analysis has predicted what kinds of interest groups are likely or unlikely to be represented in the regulatory and legislative process. It is useful to examine recent episodes of deregulation to see how well fact accords with theory. We find as expected a common theme: consumers are underrepresented. The regulatory authority must be especially careful in assessing how the interests of consumers will be affected by changes in regulation. A second theme: in those situations where some small firms and new competitors can be expected to thrive when competitive restraints are removed, their interests are not often heard.

Consider first the case of discount securities brokers. Before deregulation, of course, there were no discount brokers. Undoubtedly many brokers or people who could easily have qualified to be brokers were inclined to sell at discount prices if it were allowed. But before deregulation it was very hard to predict which brokers (or individuals) would increase market share (or successfully enter) if price competition were permitted. Although some brokers clearly have benefited from deregulation, the twin effects of large numbers and uncertainty explain why such brokers were not an effective interest group prior to deregulation.

Some consumers were at least indirectly represented in the debate over deregulation of brokerage commissions. Recipients of pensions, for example, were represented by the large institutional investors responsible for their pension funds, among other things. These large financial intermediaries perceived that they would pay lower rates under price competition and lobbied for elimination of price fixing. In contrast, small direct investors were not represented by a lobbying organization.

Consumer interests were, for a long time, perversely represented or not represented at all in the debate over deregulating telephone terminal equipment.[7] The interests of consumers in having a larger selection of higher quality terminal equipment at lower competitive prices were not adequately represented by independent outside interest groups. Indeed, such consumer interests were represented if at all only by the potential entrants. Deregulation was stalled for a time by the fears of the telephone company and some regulators that local phone rates would rise and service quality would deteriorate. AT&T and its allies among state regulators were thus able to stall beneficial regulatory reform by focusing attention on a small and chimerical fear. A measure of the degree to which subsequent deregulation benefited the public can be found in the rapidity with which AT&T customers turned to competitive sources of terminal equipment. AT&T's relative lack of success when faced with competition indicates the extent to which it either produced at inefficiently high cost or failed to take advantage of existing technology to produce state-of-the-art products with features consumers wanted prior to deregulation. Consumers' actual behavior has revealed their preference for non-AT&T products and has forced changes in AT&T's behavior. But this consumer interest was not well represented by any outside consumer interest group prior to deregulation.

Consider, as another example, the case of radio station formats. The FCC was ultimately able to deregulate radio format changes as a result of the Supreme Court decision in the *WNCN* case.[8] But in the policy debate and litigation surrounding that decision, radio listeners were not represented according to their actual stake in the outcome. Some public interest lawyers argued for retaining FCC oversight of format changes, as did representatives of listener groups organized to resist changes in the formats of particular stations. Listeners of classical music stations had an interest in opposing deregulation. But quite unrepresented were listener groups that would benefit from format changes. The problem facing such groups was that their members could not identify themselves as such. While the listener group whose favorite programs were threatened by change was easy to identify, no one could be sure what the new format or its audience would be. Moreover, to the extent that the change was predictable, the beneficiaries tended to be younger, poorer, and less well-educated, whereas listeners to the classical format tended to be the affluent and educated few. Even if the beneficiaries of deregulation could be identified, they would probably be much harder to organize.

As Joseph Kalt's case study in chapter 6 points out in greater detail, the interests of consumers were not well represented in the debates over energy price decontrol. The so-called public interest groups supported price controls on the grounds that lower prices were better and that energy companies deserved punishment. This position probably did accurately represent the short-term economic interest of some consumers. Customer groups that received all the natural gas they wanted, for example, at low controlled prices may have been net beneficiaries of energy price deregulation.

But the overall effect of energy price regulation on consumers was not beneficial. Consumers paid the world price of oil, set by the production and pricing decisions of the OPEC countries. The real effects of regulating domestic oil prices were to subsidize imports and curtail domestic oil and gas production, neither of which had been intended by the policy makers and both of which rather clearly disserved the general public interest. In addition, some producer groups (small refiners) benefited from the manner in which price regulation was administered. Small refiners became a vocal and effective interest group in opposition to deregulation.

Andrew Carron's case study in chapter 4 explains why consumer interest groups were not very influential in the debate over allowing banks and savings and loans to pay market interest rates to small savers. Small savers are very numerous, creating the free rider problem; they also individually have a small stake in the outcome of the debate. Individual small savers are thus deterred in at least two ways from forming an effective interest group. Individuals with larger amounts to invest usually take advantage of opportunities to earn market rates of interest.

Consumers similarly are underrepresented in debates on the extent and method of regulating environmental quality. Because the costs of pollution controls are passed on in product prices, consumers of manufactured products have a substantial economic stake in environmental regulation. There is obviously a trade-off between the environmental benefits from pollution control and the resulting costs imposed on consumers of manufactured products. But customers' interests in this trade-off are not represented because they are numerous and because their individual interest in particular pollution control regulations is small.

Consumers with very strong demands for environmental improvement are represented by environmental groups, but as Robert Crandall points out these groups sometimes act contrary to consumer interests because they are not accountable to consumers generally.

In surface freight deregulation, discussed more fully in the case study by Marcus Alexis in chapter 7, industry opposition among truckers and railroads gradually diminished over time. Railroads in particular came to believe that regulatory restrictions on prices, entry, and exit worked to their disadvantage. Thus by the end of the deregulation debate railroads and some contract truckers had identified themselves as likely beneficiaries of deregulation and took positions favoring it.

Consumers of freight services generally were not well represented, and public interest groups were not very active in this deregulation debate. Consumers of surface freight services in sparsely populated areas were represented only indirectly. There was the usual political concern over the prices they paid and the service they received. With regard to trucking, this concern was ill founded because no mechanism was identified that would have forced truckers to serve rural communities. Indeed, no general failure of service to rural areas has been identified following deregulation.

As discussed earlier, agriculture is a very successful industry in advocating its interests. Agricultural cooperatives administering marketing orders have been able to avoid some of the problems of large numbers and free riding one might expect them to have. Such organizations can obtain complete monopolies on marketing of specific commodities. Moreover, they can deduct their expenses before paying member farmers for goods marketed. As a result, to the extent advocacy costs are an allowable expense of the cooperative, the need to solicit voluntary contributions from individual farmers is avoided. An additional advantage of the agricultural industry is that its opponents, consumers, are numerous and thereby underrepresented as usual.

Elimination of anticompetitive regulatory practices in ocean shipping, as well as reduction or elimination of the large subsidies received by that industry, have been blocked by the industry and its unions.[9] We have already discussed some of the reasons why the industry and its unions have been successful in financing their advocacy.

Ocean freight service customers, both ultimate individual consumers and shippers, face the familiar problems of large numbers and heterogeneity in organizing their interests. Prospective challengers to the anticompetitive practices of the shipping conferences must also face the fact that foreign governments are even stronger supporters of the conferences than is our own. Diplomatic barriers thus reduce the probability of a successful reform effort, which further reduces the attractiveness of a large-scale advocacy effort.

The factors regarding the effectiveness with which interests are represented in regulatory proceedings are also apparent in the pending deregulation proposals. The FCC's proceedings on the financial and syndication interests of networks have witnessed strong, effective participation by the networks and the motion picture companies. Both are industries with major financial stakes in the outcome; both are small groups with largely homogeneous interests in the debate; and both have a long history of effective participation in political, legal, and administrative processes.

Other groups also have stakes in the proceedings, but their interests are more diffuse, subject to greater uncertainty, and spread over a larger number of heterogeneous members. Depending on the degree to which they face these problems, they can expect to be less effectively represented.

Independent or fledgling producers should prefer a marketplace characterized by the largest number of competitive buyers of program material, so they should have a stake in the issue. Their attitude toward the rules is influenced by two phenomena. First, the present group of independent producers does not include those who were eliminated (or never were able to enter) because the present rules precluded associating with a network. The rules favor existing producers over potential entrants, and potential entrants are not usually an effective interest group because their stakes are uncertain and diffuse. Second, even those independent producers who might favor rescinding the rules are heavily dependent on the major studios for financial support of current projects. They therefore have strong incentives not to risk business relations with the studios by advocating a change in the rules that may not come to pass.

Television stations affiliated with networks, their viewers, and their advertisers are currently hurt by the financial interest rule. To the extent that the rule leads to an inefficient structure of the program production industry, a given expenditure by the networks buys a lower quality program that is presumably less satisfying to viewers.[10] As a result, audiences are less attracted to network television. This in turn injures advertisers to the extent the rules divert audiences to pay-TV, which does not have advertising, or to nonbroadcast leisure activities.

Independent stations probably have a short-run interest in opposing repeal of the financial interest rule. If repeal improves network programming, network affiliates will capture audiences from independents. Eventually, however, both affiliated stations and independents should realize long-term benefits as higher quality programming appears in syndication.

All of these effects, of course, are of a smaller magnitude than the stakes perceived by networks and motion picture companies in their competition for financial interests in successful programs. In every case the stakes are spread over a larger number of participants than the small number of networks and movie studios. Moreover, the situations of different stations, viewers, and advertisers will vary substantially. For example, the ability of network television to compete effectively with pay-TV is an important issue only in areas with extensive cable or Subscription Television (STV) development now or on the near horizon. Among advertisers, the stakes differ according to the kinds of audiences sought, level of broadcast (national or local), and demographic characteristics. We would doubt, for example, that Bible publishers who buy advertising on independent stations featuring religious programming would perceive much stake in the current financial interest and syndication proceedings.

The preceding analysis suggests the following conclusions about whose interests should be represented in the FCC's proceedings about network syndication rights. None of the groups discussed above should be represented as effectively as networks and motion picture companies. Television stations as a group have more heterogeneous interests and will thus not speak with one voice. Some affiliated stations have important syndication interests and therefore have an interest in keeping the networks out of syndication. Some independent stations may perceive that their long-term interests lie with greater competition in syndication markets.

An even more heterogeneous group is the advertisers. They have even smaller stakes than the stations, because simple shifts in audience from one category of stations to another will not be an important matter to many of them. A few large advertisers or industry groups that collectively advertise a great deal may be moved to participate to a small degree. They are already organized to keep abreast of FCC proceedings that may affect them and may want to be sure that their perceptions of small stakes are correct, but they are unlikely to exert much influence.

Finally, consumers of advertised products and television viewers are essentially unrepresented. Their interests are heterogeneous and their numbers large. Collectively speaking, they may have large stakes in the matter to the extent that product prices and program quality will be affected by the outcome, but individually these stakes are most likely to be very small. Viewers and consumers are passive customers—they have no direct dealings with program producers or even broadcasters, other than to select channels, and therefore have no reason to be informed about the intricate processes of the industry that determine program quality. They are thus not likely to perceive whatever small stakes they may have. For all of these reasons, we would expect not only viewers but also their surrogate representatives, consumer groups, to ignore these proceedings.

Worth noting is that the interests of three groups most likely to benefit from competition in programming—the advertisers, viewers, and those program producers who do not exist but would if networks could finance programming—are also least likely to be represented. Arguments favoring competition in regulatory policy will therefore be supplied by only two sources: the networks, who in this case have an interest in promoting competition, and the FCC itself, which bears the responsibility for ensuring that diffuse, general public interests are duly considered.

Notes

1. *The Federalist Papers* (New York: Mentor, 1961), pp. 78-79.

2. Cable television deregulation is surveyed in Bruce Owen, "The Rise and Fall of Cable Television Regulation," in Leonard W. Weiss and Michael W. Klass, eds., *Case Studies in Regulation* (Boston: Little, Brown, 1981).

3. Deregulation of securities brokers' commission rates is discussed in Hans Stoll, "Revolution in the Regulation of Securities Markets" in Weiss and Klass, eds., *Case Studies in Regulation*; William F. Baxter, "NYSE Fixed Commission Rates: A Private Cartel Goes Public," *Stanford Law Review*, vol. 22 (1970), p. 675; Lawrence G. Goldberg and Lawrence J. White, eds., *The Deregulation of the Banking and Securities Industries* (Lexington, Mass.: D.C. Heath, 1979).

4. A history of technological change, regulation, and dominant firm strategy in intercity telecommunications is presented in Gerald Brock, *The Telecommunications Industry: The Dynamics of Market Structure* (Cambridge: Harvard University Press, 1981), pp. 170-233, 254-86.

5. The Consumer Product Safety Commission's bicycle safety standard is discussed in Nina Cornell, Roger Noll, and Barry Weingast, "Safety Regulation," in Henry Owen and Charles Schultze, eds., *Setting National Priorities* (Washington, D.C.: Brookings, 1976).

6. The "free rider" problem is discussed in Mancur Olson, *The Logic of Collective Action* (Cambridge, Mass.: Harvard University Press, 1965).

7. Deregulation of the telephone customer equipment business is discussed in Gerald Brock, *The Telecommunications Industry*, pp. 234-53, and in a majority staff report of the Subcommittee on Telecommunications of the House Committee on Energy and Commerce, "Telecommunications in Transition," (1981), pp. 184-94. See also the two major opinions of U.S. District Court Judge Harold Green in United States v. AT&T, 524 F. Supp. 1336, 1348-52 (1981); 43 Antitrust and Trade Regulation Report S-1, S-58 (1982).

8. The Supreme Court decision permitting FCC deregulation of radio station format changes is FCC v. WNCN Listeners' Guild, 450 U.S. 582 (1981). The FCC decision to deregulate radio more generally is reported at 46 Fed. Reg. 13888 (Feb. 24, 1981).

9. Maritime Regulation is covered by Gerald Jantscher, *Bread upon the Waters: Federal Aids to the Maritime Industry* (Washington, D.C.: Brookings, 1975) and Robert Larner, "Public Policy in the Ocean Freight Industry," in Almarin Phillips, ed., *Promoting Competition in Regulated Markets* (Washington, D.C.: Brookings, 1975).

10. Program quality as used here refers to the cost and value of technical and talent resources used in production, rather than subjective judgments reflecting personal aesthetic tastes.

3
The Predictability of Interest Group Arguments

As chapters 1 and 2 have shown, the act of regulating an industry can create new special interests and enhance the wealth of other groups. The financial or other interests of both types of groups are furthered by maintaining regulation. These interest groups have incentives to behave strategically in using the regulatory process itself to preserve regulation. It is striking that many of the proregulation arguments and tactics of special interest groups recur in different regulatory contexts. Much of this strategic behavior has been shown in a number of regulatory settings to be entirely self-serving. Many of the dire predictions made by opponents of deregulation have proven false in practice.

In this chapter we survey a number of general strategies and arguments available to interest groups that benefit from regulation. Each strategy has been used before different regulatory bodies. Where possible we also assess specific evidence from different industries regarding the validity of the arguments used to oppose deregulation.

Destructive Competition

A common argument made by interest groups favoring regulation is that unregulated competition will destroy the competitive process with cutthroat practices. This will drive out competitors, leaving only a few dominant survivors who then will be able to gouge consumers, even though the economics of production exhibit insufficient scale economies to constitute a natural monopoly. Applied to the case of network interests in program production, the argument is that networks will eventually drive out other production sources or syndicators by practicing cutthroat competition. Similar arguments are made by title insurance companies in opposing repeal of section 8 of the Real Estate Settlement Practices Act and by maritime interests in their effort to gain further antitrust immunity for their cartels.

Fear of destructive competition was the dominant rationale for much of the economic regulation enacted in the 1930s. Airlines, trucking, and agriculture are leading examples of industries in which extensive government control of prices and production capacity was introduced because competition was then thought to be the source of severe economic problems. Of course, the 1930s were also the years of the most severe depression in the history of the United States. Widespread bankruptcies and economic dislocation were the norm; some industries were just more successful than others in obtaining political acquiescence in the creation of anticompetitive policies. Indeed, had the Supreme Court not declared the National Recovery Act unconstitutional, the Great Depression would very likely have left a legacy of anticompetitive regulation for almost every important industry in the country. Forty years of history and economic research have taught us that the causes of recessions and depressions are not found in the competitive structure of individual markets. The regulation created in the 1930s not only was ineffective in coping with the Great Depression, but, when based upon the rationale of destructive competition, led to inefficiencies when recovery did take place.

Still, the destructive competition concept remains alive and well in regulatory proceedings, where it is today most commonly used as an argument against deregulation. The many applications of this argument before various regulatory bodies rarely contain a coherent articulation of the conditions leading to destructive competition. This is not surprising. Competition is most effective in producing efficiency and serving consumer interests when it is not hampered by regulatory restrictions. A circumstance in which destructive competition could be documented as the cause of poor performance in an industry has seldom if ever been observed.

In the debate over deregulation proposals, the destructive competition argument normally takes the following form. First, the argument is made that deregulation will threaten some significant fraction of firms with bankruptcy. Second, the proponents of regulation assert that this, on balance, will harm consumers by causing fewer firms to compete for their services.

The first part of the argument is often valid. Recall that regulation creates special interests whose welfare depends on its continuation. If regulators try to prop up inefficient companies by giving them favorable rulings, these firms are quite likely to fail if deregulation forces them to compete with efficient firms. In the case of airlines, regulation led to circumstances in which companies differed by as much as 100 percent in their costs of serving similar routes and in which some companies had been given far stronger route structures than others. Consequently, deregulation—especially in the teeth of the nation's worst economic setback since the Great Depression—has led to a restructuring of the industry through bankruptcies and mergers.

The second part of the destructive competition argument is incorrect, and indeed illogical. If regulation permits some inefficient firms to survive, and deregulation causes these firms to be replaced by more efficient firms charging lower prices, the interests of consumers are hardly threatened. Indeed, one source of the advantage of competition to consumers is that it weeds out the inefficient companies, allowing only the efficient to prosper. As Joseph Kalt's analysis in chapter 6 indicates, the economy paid a high price to prop up inefficient small refineries with regulatory subsidies. These refineries yielded expensive mixes of petroleum products and thwarted achievement of environmental goals.

The destructive competition argument also ignores the tendency of regulation to preclude the entry of new companies that promise to serve consumers better than the incumbents. While deregulation may have led to the disappearance of Braniff and the merger of Continental with Texas International, it also permitted the development of new, low-cost carriers like Capitol, the extension of a regional carrier to national status in the case of Republic, and the expansion of some very efficient intrastate carriers into regional ones, like PSA. In fact, regulation can lead to fewer firms. The number of inefficient companies that are protected may be smaller than the number of efficient companies that are not allowed to enter. Evidence in support of this view includes the dramatic reduction in the numbers of trucking, railroad, and airline firms in the postwar era because of the promotion of mergers by the Interstate Commerce Commission and the Civil Aeronautics Board.

The second step of the destructive competition argument in any event ignores the true definition of competition. Competition is not measured by the number of companies in an industry, but by the extent to which a company (or a group of firms exhibiting cooperative behavior) has a protected position in the markets it serves. Even if regulation leads to more companies in total than competition does, it also divides markets so that competition among companies is restricted. Regulation slows and sometimes consciously prevents entry of new firms and limits the number of companies that are allowed to serve a particular market. Indeed, until the 1970s, most economic regulation required that a potential entrant prove that the incumbents were not serving a market adequately in order to achieve permission to enter, and the proof had to exclude arguments based upon price.

True competition—the kind that is in the interests of consumers— exists when a firm that tries to charge excessive prices, that offers a poor quality of service, or that has high prices because it is inefficient finds that other firms expand or enter by offering lower prices or better service. The number of companies in an industry is a poor measure of true competition. Better measures take account of structural conditions affecting the incentives to compete or cooperate and the number of firms that could relatively easily enter if the incumbents did not charge competitive prices.

The airline example illustrates the invalidity of the destructive competition argument for preserving regulation. Deregulation may have been destructive in the sense that it contributed to the demise of some carriers, but it also increased true competition. Deregulation increased operating efficiency, rationalized route structures, and, when corrections are made for inflation and fuel costs, dramatically lowered prices.

Airlines are not the only example of the demonstrated inaccuracy of the destructive competition argument. One of the clearest examples is the support by the New York Stock Exchange (NYSE) of fixed commission rates for securities brokerage services. Prior to their abolition in 1975, fixed commissions resulted in prices for brokerage services that were significantly above costs for many transactions. These cartelized prices were supported by various rules and regulations that effectively prevented competition among member firms.

The NYSE justified regulation of commission rates in part by asserting that the cost structure of providing brokerage services would lead to destructive competition without a regulatory regime to control prices. The exchange alleged that economies of scale and a high ratio of fixed to variable costs would lead to monopolization of the industry or dominance by a few large firms if commission rates were not fixed.

The evidence presented by the NYSE in support of its contentions concerning the costs of providing brokerage services was effectively criticized by advocates of deregulation. But the real proof has been the experience with competitive commission rates since 1975. While the very largest firms have increased their share of commission revenues, this continues a trend that started well before competitive commission rates were in effect. In fact, the trend has slowed since deregulation. More important, hundreds of brokerage firms still survive, and many of the innovators offering discount brokerage services to small investors have been small brokerage firms.

Experience has shown the destructive competition argument of the NYSE to be spurious. It was used merely to support a cartelized price structure. Since the abolition of fixed rates, commission charges have fallen on average by 15 percent according to the Securities and

Exchange Commission, saving consumers about $400 million annually.

Similar arguments concerning excessive or destructive competition have been made to support the continued regulation of trucking, banking, and ocean shipping. The arguments have no greater theoretical appeal for these industries than they did for the securities and airline industries. But because deregulation has not proceeded very far in these industries, direct empirical evidence to refute the destructive competition argument is sparse. The exception is shipment of agricultural commodities by trucks, which was deregulated successfully in the 1950s. Like airlines and securities, the trucking, banking, and ocean shipping industries are structurally competitive. No legitimate theoretical argument can be made that these industries would not be workably competitive in the absence of regulation. And like airlines and securities, the continuation of regulation in these industries maintains high prices and restricted entry, to the ultimate detriment of consumers. The costs imposed on shippers by trucking regulation alone have been estimated at several billion dollars.

A politically appealing variant of the destructive competition argument is that competition will harm or eliminate a particular (and powerful) group or class of competitors. Proponents may concede that the favored group is less efficient, but will argue that there are valid social reasons to protect it anyway. Agricultural marketing orders are classic examples of anticompetitive practices defended on the basis of such arguments—in this case, ensuring the survival of the family farm.

Marketing orders restrict output so that prices will rise above competitive levels. Two points about this policy should be made. First, whatever benefit it brings by supporting small farmers is enormously expensive to consumers. Dairy regulation alone has been estimated to cost consumers hundreds of millions of dollars annually. Second, the targeted group, small farmers, does not receive the bulk of the benefits from higher agricultural prices. Marketing orders increase prices for all, large and small alike. And if the favored group is inefficient, regulation will thereby enhance the profits of the ostensibly unfavored but efficient producers by even more than it benefits the favored ones. In some instances, small farmers may even have suffered while larger farmers were enriched. Controls on milk marketing, for example, divide dairy operators into two classes, A and B, according to whether their milk meets standards for consumption in fluid form.[1] It has been estimated that milk marketing orders benefit Grade A producers at the expense of both consumers and Grade B producers. But Grade B operators are almost uniformly smaller farms. The lesson here is not to mistake the true identity of an interest group that has a stake in an anticompetitive policy.

Elimination of Desirable Cross-Subsidies

The Federal Communications Commission originally installed the rules barring network acquisition of property rights in programs on the hypothesis that the rules would provide producers with the financial wherewithal to enter the first-run syndication market, in which producers bypass networks and sell directly to stations. The idea, apparently, was that studios and independent producers will use the extra revenues allegedly available to them from off-network sales to finance production of entirely different programs that bypass the networks.

Whatever the merits, if any, of this logic, the cross-subsidy argument is a familiar one in deregulation debates. The idea is that regulation results in desirable cross-subsidies that will be eliminated by deregulation. That is, a particular (presumably deserving) class of consumers has been charged lower prices as a result of subsidies from higher prices charged to other customers. Proponents of regulation have an incentive to create (or to claim to have created) cross-subsidies that could never exist in a competitive market. The reason is that such cross-subsidies lead to new special interest groups, the beneficiaries of the (alleged) cross-subsidy, which have an economic stake in the preservation of the status quo. As a result, the elimination of perceived cross-subsidies can create a substantial political barrier to deregulation.

Often the cross-subsidies are more alleged than real. The airline industry presents an excellent example of this particular phenomenon. As we have seen, some interests opposed deregulation in part by asserting that deregulation would result in loss of service to smaller communities. The contention was that regulation protected higher prices on high density routes, the revenues from which supported service on low density routes. The airlines were never able to present convincing evidence that this cross-subsidy was significant or even that it existed at all.

Judge Stephen Breyer reports the experience during the 1975 Kennedy hearings of trying to pin down the airlines about exactly which cities would lose service if deregulation was undertaken. The number of allegedly threatened markets dwindled nearly to zero as more data were acquired.[2]

The experience since deregulation has shown that service to small communities has not suffered. While the total number of departures at small airports has declined slightly, the number of flights between small airports and larger airports has increased. The substitution of flights between small towns by flights between small towns and major cities has probably increased the value of air service to small communities. The prior structure of service was created by route awards by regulators, whereas the current structure is in response to the pattern of consumer demand. Presumably the willingness of consumers to pay in a competitive market is a better measure of their interests.

Similar arguments have been made by some segments of the trucking industry in opposition to trucking deregulation. They maintain that service to small communities has been subsidized and will be eliminated or its price increased under deregulation. Considerable contrary evidence exists that the provision of trucking service to small communities is and would remain profitable. Whatever the merits of either side, simply raising the issue increased the political opposition to deregulation and increased the burden on those who would deregulate. Opponents of deregulation had an incentive to raise the issue regardless of its validity.

The cross-subsidy argument has also been used extensively by AT&T to maintain regulation and to prevent competition. AT&T fought the decisions of the Federal Communications Commission providing for a competitive terminal equipment industry in part by arguing that monopoly provision of such equipment was subsidizing basic telephone service. The argument automatically produced political support for AT&T's position from state regulators who were concerned with keeping local telephone rates low. AT&T was never able to provide convincing evidence that the alleged cross-subsidy even existed. Moreoever, it is widely perceived that the FCC's decision to allow competitive sale of terminal equipment has been a success, resulting in lower prices and a much greater range of options for consumers.

Excessive Risk

Groups interested in preserving regulation have said that regulation avoids unwarranted risks of physical harm to the public and the work force. Safety and health regulation are obvious examples, as is environmental regulation. The debate has been over what form regulation should take in order to achieve the goals of a safe workplace and a clean environment.

Recent debate in the safety and environmental fields has focused on the possibility of implementing market incentives and the establishment of general targets and performance standards in place of specific regulations and design standards that mandate particular processes on a plant-by-plant basis. The aim of regulatory reform is to achieve a given overall target of safety and health at lower cost. Opposition to this reform has been by some environmental and consumer groups who appear to distrust giving any discretion to firms in complying with standards. The specter of environmental hazards and unsafe workplaces is held out in opposition to reform.

At least in areas in which health and safety are the primary purpose of regulation, the debate over standards versus incentives is about means to a common end. In other areas, its connection to regulatory purposes is remote at best. The threat of excessive risks of physical harm has also been employed in economic regulatory contexts by industry groups in attempts to prevent competitive entry and deregulation.

The established drug industry has opposed the relaxation of state regulations that hinder the use of low-priced generic drugs. One argument has been that the substitution of generic drugs will increase the probability of consumption of lower quality products, which in turn could affect the health of consumers.

Some segments of the airline industry argued in a similar vein that airline deregulation and competition would result in less safe operations. In this industry, experience with deregulation has proven its opponents wrong. Statistics on air fatality rates for scheduled airlines after deregulation was legislated in 1978 indicate that deregulation has not resulted in a decrease in air-travel safety. The air fatality rate for scheduled carriers in 1979 was within the range found during the previous decade, while the 1980 and 1981 rates were extraordinarily low.

Finally, the telephone industry argued that competition in the market for terminal equipment would increase the risk of electrocution of telephone company personnel (as well as harm the telephone network). This argument was used to justify AT&T's total prohibition of such attachments. The FCC's registration and type acceptance program for terminal equipment has adequately protected telephone workers without outlawing competition.

Harm to Consumers

A major argument used to oppose deregulation has been that consumers will suffer from the absence of regulation. Arguments concerning consumer losses have taken two general forms: prices will increase under deregulation, and the quality of the goods and services will decline.

The threat of obscene profits was used to oppose deregulation of both natural gas wellhead prices and domestic oil prices. It is still used in the context of further gas price deregulation. Regulation in both industries has caused substantial inefficiencies. Shortages existed for natural gas because the market was not allowed to clear under regulation. Customers who could not obtain gas and who were willing to pay the market price for it could obtain little solace from the fact that other consumers were receiving a bargain. Moreover, the gas production industry is structured competitively. Net losses to the economy were certain by preventing gas prices from rising to competitive levels. Oil regulation similarly discouraged domestic production and encouraged imports of foreign oil. The byzantine oil regulations actually subsidized imports, thereby serving to prop up world oil prices and preventing increased competition from domestic sources. In both cases decontrol was made difficult because some consumers received benefits, or thought they did, from artificially low prices.

Similar arguments, such as the realization of lower prices and the prevention of obscene profits, have been made in favor of rent control laws. Yet proponents of rent control laws seem to ignore the effects of regulations that prevent rental prices from rising to market clearing levels. Shortages occur because at artificially low prices not enough housing is provided. Investment in rental units is discouraged, and incentives are created to convert rental properties into condominiums or other uses that are allowed to earn a market rate of return. As a result, rent control laws defeat their purpose. Rental units are not available to all those who want them at a price that earns landlords a competitive rate of return.[3]

Other opponents of deregulation argue that competition will lower the quality of service. Professions such as law, medicine, and engineering have a long history of self-regulation involving restrictions on advertising, fixed price schedules, and entry barriers.[4] The argument in favor of such constraints is that they are necessary to prevent shoddy, discount services being offered to consumers who are incapable of knowing in advance whether service will be adequate. Of course, all of these self-regulation schemes have the effect of limiting competition and supporting the incomes of current members of the respective professional groups.

One of the grounds on which the securities industry opposed the elimination of fixed commission rates was that quality of services provided by member firms of the New York Stock Exchange would deteriorate. It was alleged that without fixed commissions member firms would not provide sufficient capacity to handle peak demands and would not incur the costs of running the exchange, thereby fragmenting the market and reducing liquidity. In addition it was argued that research and other aspects of service would diminish, and small investors would be discriminated against because of their inability to negotiate lower rates.

These evils have not materialized under competition. The abolition of fixed rates removed the previous incentive to circumvent the NYSE so that the big board has been used *more* for NYSE-listed stocks since competition, thereby *reducing* fragmentation. There is no evidence of any deterioration in liquidity or market quality since 1975, and it has become clear that those providing research can be compensated without fixed commissions by charging for their counseling services. Finally, the abolition of fixed commission rates removed the economic discrimination against institutional investors without raising prices to individual investors above costs.

The broadcasting industry used a similar argument in opposing competition from new technologies. Both cable television and pay-TV (whether on cable or over-the-air) were argued to be threats to the quality of television offered to over-the-air viewers by undermining the audience for local stations. The essence of the argument was that viewers were better off with fewer viewing options because more competition would lead to poorer quality programs as well as payment for programs previously received free.

These arguments had a self-serving component. Artificial FCC limits on the spectrum allocated to broadcasting had restricted entry and made television stations very profitable. Moreover, the new services were most severely restricted in the largest cities, where over-the-air television was extremely profitable and therefore most resilient to competition.

After more than a decade of restricting new television technologies, the FCC undertook extensive reviews of the arguments supporting regulation. It found no consumer interest in preserving the restrictions and proceeded to deregulate cable and pay-TV substantially and to permit new low-power television stations and direct satellite broadcasting. This deregulation has not been in place long enough to provide a clear test of the validity of the broadcasters' case. But thus far, expansion of cable television has created several new specialized national networks in news and sports constructed around cable television systems and some independent over-the-air stations, and pay-TV has created an important new source of revenue for motion pictures and television programs. We are not aware of any local station that has gone under. Indeed, there are thousands of applications for television licenses pending at the commission.

The Incentive to Withhold or Distort Information

The history of network television regulation, new drug licensing, clean air standards, and energy regulation contains many instances of regulators seeking industry data as a basis for policy analysis. The industry groups respond with varying degrees of candor and completeness to these requests, as their interests dictate. As new deregulation debates unfold, the parties once again will have an opportunity to back their rhetoric with hard facts. Their willingness to do so is one measure of the validity of their arguments.

Many claims concerning the effects of regulation can be verified (except through deregulation) only by access to information in the hands of those with an interest in maintaining regulation. But interest groups have an incentive to withhold information that is inconsistent with their position and to present incomplete or biased information that supports their views. The ability to control relevant information applies to many of the arguments made by interest groups discussed previously.

Cross-subsidy arguments are a prime example. The most direct evidence tends to be in the hands of the groups who argue that such subsidies exist. Claims that service to certain groups or routes does not cover costs could be verified if the industry made available the relevant data. Claims of cross-subsidy without accurate evidence should create suspicion about the validity of the claim.

The airlines asserted that regulation resulted in cross-subsidized service to small communities. Some of the studies presented to justify this claim were so seriously flawed as to call into question whether cross-subsidies were significant at all. United Airlines originally asserted it would discontinue service to 75 of its 327 city pairs. When pressed to present the profitability data that would support this prediction, United had to back off. Only 29 city pairs could be justified as potential beneficiaries of cross-subsidy, and they accounted for only one half of one percent of United's total domestic revenue passenger miles. Even this was an overstatement of the loss of service to be expected from deregulation. Many unprofitable routes could be operated profitably by other lines or by altering route structures.

AT&T similarly has consistently failed to provide credible evidence to support its claims that competition in the telephone industry would be detrimental to consumers. The allegation that cross-subsidies to local service would be ended by competition for terminal equipment has never been adequately documented. Likewise AT&T's assertion that it enjoys substantial economies of scale in the provision of intercity services has not been demonstrated. Yet, if true, it should have been possible for AT&T to provide convincing evidence.

The airline industry also tended to ignore other relevant evidence in supporting continued regulation. Intrastate airlines in California and Texas were not subject to rigid federal regulation. Fares in those states for intrastate flights were significantly lower than for equivalent interstate flights under CAB regulation. The industry tried to dismiss this evidence as special cases but could not, when pressed, explain away the differences in fares.

For advocates of deregulation to disprove claims about the social benefits of regulation is usually extremely difficult. Sometimes it is impossible. The relevant information is usually in the hands of the regulated industry, with its interest in preserving regulation. Once the industry is successful in raising an issue like cross-subsidization or economies of scale, it can delay deregulation because the industry's opponents have little direct ammunition to rebut the claims. Policy makers must proceed on the basis of theoretical arguments.

Conclusions about Regulatory Strategies and Tactics

Chapters 2 and 3 argue that among numerous, quite disparate regulatory policy debates a certain consistency or pattern emerges. There is regularity in the selective way in which interests are represented in the process. There are certain identifiable economic interests of regulated firms, suppliers, and customers that actually can be more effectively pursued under an umbrella of protective regulation than in a free, competitive market. Moreover, there is regularity in the types of arguments that are used to merge special interest pleadings with a more general public interest and in the choice of tactics for influencing regulatory policy.

The regulatory process is much like the adversary system as a means for reaching decisions under conditions of opposing interests. When the adversary system involves a bilateral conflict with little if any spillovers to third parties, advocates of each side can be expected between them to provide a relatively complete range of arguments and facts on which a reasonably informed decision can be made. And even if they do not provide adequate information, the principal cost of a bad decision is borne by the advocates themselves. The regulatory process, however, is rarely concerned with narrow issues affecting only well-represented interests in direct conflict. Indeed, agencies have the mandate—and usually the internal resources—to make certain that all relevant arguments and facts are considered and to reach a conclusion that is justified on principles of general public purpose. Not surprisingly, then, well-represented interests attempt to perform this function for the agency by identifying their narrow concerns with the larger, more diffuse interests that remain unrepresented. Indeed, they can be especially inventive in thinking of arguments to relate consumer interests to the quest for special protections.

In these introductory chapters we have illustrated these general tendencies by a series of references to specific issues in specific regulatory policies. These examples, while useful as illustrations of the general argument, by themselves are not sufficiently comprehensive to make the point that we seek to stress: the regularity and predictability in debates about regulatory reform, especially with respect to arguments that camouflage anticompetitive aims.

The following chapters provide detailed histories of several deregulation proceedings. Each describes the roles of various interest groups in the process that eventually produced (or failed to produce) substantial reforms. Each is written from the perspective of the conceptual model of interest group representation described in the beginning chapters in this book. They provide the more comprehensive treatment that is necessary to make our general point.

Notes

1. Milk marketing orders are discussed in Paul MacAvoy, ed., *Federal Milk Marketing Orders and Price Supports* (Washington, D.C.: American Enterprise Institute, 1977).
2. Stephen Breyer, *Regulation and Its Reform* (Cambridge, Mass.: Harvard University Press, 1981), chap. 16.
3. The economics of rent controls are discussed in Paul Samuelson, *Economics*, 11th ed. (New York: McGraw-Hill, 1980), pp. 369-70.
4. Regulation of the professions is discussed by several authors in Simon Rottenberg, ed., *Occupational Licensure and Regulation* (Washington, D.C.: American Enterprise Institute, 1980), and in Roger D. Blair and Stephen Rubin, eds., *Regulating the Professions* (Lexington, Mass.: D.C. Heath, 1980).

PART TWO

4

The Political Economy
of Financial Regulation

ANDREW S. CARRON

The modern structure of financial regulation in the United States has its origins in the Great Depression. Federal deposit insurance, the Securities and Securities Exchange acts, the Federal Home Loan Bank System, and the mutual fund industry are products of that era. Laws and regulations dating from that period succeeded in restoring the soundness and viability of the financial system and served the country well for many years. Now, as a result of changing economic conditions and the financial market innovations they spawned, much of the existing legal structure has been called into question. The rules in place for the past half-century have not only become outmoded and cumbersome, they have also had the unintended effect of creating preferences and subsidies for certain groups in the economy.

A key to understanding the history of financial regulation is the distinction between the goals sought and the practices employed. Safety and soundness were paramount considerations. These could have been achieved through simply establishing rules for behavior— requiring disclosure, prohibiting insider transactions, compelling independent audits. Firms were also to be limited to a single kind of business, so there was no direct competition among banks, savings institutions, and securities firms, only between firms of the same type. This lack of competition was one of the chosen means of providing safety.

The promotion of particular social goals, such as increasing the availability of housing, was also important. Restrictions on the activities of particular types of firms were intended to serve as the mecha-

NOTE: The author is senior fellow in the Economic Studies Program of the Brookings Institution. The views expressed here are those of the author and should not be attributed to the trustees, officers, or other staff members of the Brookings Institution.

nism of this policy as well. Direct subsidies could have been used to accomplish these objectives, but indirect means were selected. Such indirect subsidies have invariably proved less efficient in achieving desired public goals, but as frequently they have been the more attractive politically.

A result of this pattern of regulation was a system that, by the 1960s, was well established and safe but marked by rigid distinctions among types of institutions. Commercial banks could offer checking accounts and loans to commercial customers but could operate only in a single state. Savings institutions paid higher rates of interest but were not permitted to provide checking accounts. Securities dealers could operate across state lines, although they were foreclosed from accepting deposits.

By the 1970s, market forces and innovation had begun to erode the intent of regulations. Traditional barriers began to break down. The response, however, was not to make the regulatory system more flexible and more competitive. Instead, incumbent firms and others with a stake in the preexisting system pressed for more regulation, preservation of existing distinctions, and tighter enforcement. Only recently, in the context of a regulatory reform movement ranging across product and service industries, have there been attempts at comprehensive reform in the regulation of financial markets.

In this chapter, I will review three major regulations that together span the major issues in financial regulation:

1. rate ceilings on time and savings accounts, which permitted depository institutions to pay consumers less than the going market rate of interest at a time when small savers had few other investment opportunities

2. limitations on the investment powers of savings institutions, which allowed smaller commercial banks to have monopolies on commercial and agricultural lending and on checking accounts in many parts of the country

3. restrictions on the powers of banks, which have given the securities industry the exclusive right to sell mutual fund shares to the public and underwrite the revenue bonds of state and local governments, thus limiting competition

A discussion of these regulations will illustrate how rules affecting prices, products, and market entry can create and maintain preferences that do not serve the broad public interest. The debates persisted for a dozen years before the impact on consumers became too large to ignore. Only then did the impetus to reform begin.

ANDREW S. CARRON

Deposit Rate Ceilings

Government regulation has helped to hold the cost of funds to depository institutions below the market rate of interest. Since 1933 the Federal Reserve Board's Regulation Q has set the maximum rates that commercial banks are allowed to pay on time and savings deposits. These ceilings were raised along with market rates and so were generally not binding constraints until 1966. Rates at savings institutions, until then not subject to rate ceilings, were slightly higher than at commercial banks.

In 1966 there was a fundamental change of policy. At that time, deposit rate ceilings were extended to thrift institutions (savings and loan associations, mutual savings banks, and credit unions). And the permissible rates were pegged at a level below the market rate of interest. Despite periodic increases, these rate maxima generally remained below market rates until 1978, and some controls remain even today.

A major effect of the rate ceilings was to reduce the cost of the institutions' liabilities. The controls were intended to promote housing policy by improving the profitability of lending institutions and by making it possible for them to offer cheaper mortgages. In fact, however, there is scant evidence that the low-cost deposits were ever passed through to mortgage borrowers (see figure 4–1).[1] Lenders without access to these deposits—mortgage bankers, insurance companies, and others—made about one-third of the new mortgage loans during the period of rate controls. Since they had to obtain funds in competition with other borrowers such as corporations and the federal government, their mortgage loan rates were (and are) determined by the market as a whole. Thrifts never accounted for much more than half of the housing loans, so they asked for and received the same market rates.

What the rate controls accomplished was higher profits for savings institutions. The after-tax income of savings associations declined from 1.0 percent of average assets in the early 1960s to less than 0.5 percent by the time rate controls were applied. Profits then immediately recovered, reaching 0.8 percent in 1978, the year controls began to come off. The institutions also used their extra income from market-rate mortgages and low-cost deposits to raise salaries, hire more employees, and construct new offices for themselves.[2] In the period before deposit rate controls, the assets of savings and loan associations grew one-third faster than their operating expenses. When deposit rate ceilings sheltered the firms from competition, expense growth

FIGURE 4–1

INTEREST RATES ON MORTGAGES, BONDS, AND SAVINGS, 1953–1978

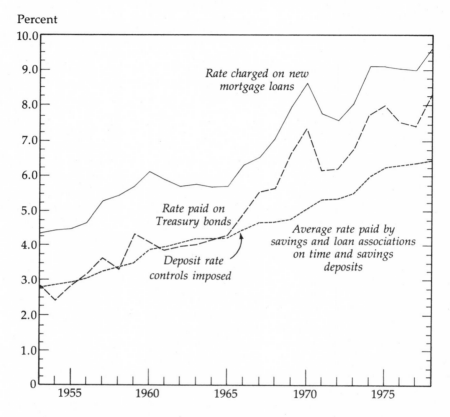

Percent

NOTES: Effective rate charged on conventional mortgage loans for purchase of new homes adjusted by the author for changes in duration; yield on U.S. Treasury securities adjusted to ten-year constant maturity; average yield on time and savings deposits at FHLBB-member savings and loan associations.
SOURCES: *Economic Report of the President,* 1981, table B-65; Federal Home Loan Bank Board, *Savings and Home Financing Sourcebook: 1980,* 1981, pp. 30, 61.

outpaced asset growth by one-third.[3] As most associations have "mutual" charters, there are no private stockholders to whom the extra earnings could be paid. Thus amenities such as those mentioned here were the only means the companies had for realizing tangible benefits from their favorable positions.

There were periodic attempts by some competitive banks to get the ceilings raised during the 1970s, but the other depository institutions successfully blocked these moves.[4] The thrift industry argued that because it had become dependent on low-cost deposits, it would be harmed by the removal of ceilings. They claimed, spuriously, that below-market deposits were helping to subsidize the mortgage market. Further, representatives of the savings institutions raised the specter of a rate war that would risk the safety of deposits, even though they were insured by an entity of the federal government.[5] So as market rates rose from about 5 percent in the mid-1960s to above 10 percent by the late 1970s, the maximum rate payable on savings deposits was lifted from 4¾ percent to 5¼ percent. Rate ceilings were higher on some time deposits, but these too were generally below market rates. Throughout the 1970s, the average rate was depressed on all types of deposits at thrift institutions.

Deposit rate ceilings did not affect all consumers equally. Wealthy individuals with $100,000 or more to invest were not covered by the controls after 1970. Customers with somewhat smaller amounts—$10,000 to $25,000, for example—could buy Treasury bills and bonds at market rates. But the small saver had no alternative to the closely regulated accounts at depository institutions.[6]

The proponents of continued rate ceilings overlooked the changed circumstances that increasingly invalidated their arguments. Higher interest rates were being made available to individuals. Competition was developing outside the depository institutions, particularly in the form of money market mutual funds, although Treasury bills and corporate notes were also attractive to investors. Thus recent debates saw the depository institutions proposing that rates on the competing unregulated investments be reduced.[7] The thrift industry suggested that rates on money market mutual funds be limited by imposing rate ceilings or reserve requirements. Rather than making savings deposits more attractive to consumers, the industry wanted to make the alternatives less so.

By 1982, the depository institutions still held nearly $500 billion in accounts subject to below-market rate ceilings.[8] They had a vested interest in perpetuating these regulations. It was estimated that decontrol would increase interest payments to depositors by at least $20 billion per year.[9] Yet complete decontrol has still not taken place, despite the obvious advantages to the public.

The answer may perhaps lie in the fact that the nation's 4,500 savings institutions and 11,000 small banks are well-organized interest groups with strong trade associations. Their concern is direct and apparent. On the other side of the equation are the tens of millions of account holders to whom the difference between continued regulation and reform may be only a few dollars a month.

A significant degree of deposit rate decontrol has occurred since 1978. Ceilings on accounts at credit unions have been entirely removed. Most funds at other depository institutions reside in new types of accounts tied to (but usually somewhat below) market rates of interest. Recent experience therefore provides a partial test of the claims made by opponents of deregulation.

The cost to savings institutions has indeed gone up: The average depositor now earns about 11¼ percent compared with 6½ percent in 1978.[10] But contrary to predictions, mortgage and other loan rates have not risen out of line with long-term rates generally. The rate on new mortgages was 1.6 percentage points higher than the rate on comparable Treasury bonds in 1977 (the year before the beginning of decontrol). Since then, the premium on mortgages has ranged from 1.2 to 1.5 percentage points.[11]

Nor has there been a destructive "rate war," as many institutions are choosing to pay less than the ceiling rates on some deposits. On the small saver certificate, for which the ceiling rate closely approximates the market rate, 55 percent of commercial banks, 73 percent of mutual savings banks, and 52 percent of savings and loan associations are paying less than the maximum allowed by law.[12]

Consumers have clearly benefited. They have poured hundreds of billions of dollars into these new accounts—more than double the amount that has gone into money market mutual funds—and they are now earning higher rates of interest. Community banks have survived in this less-regulated environment, and thrift institutions are still finding profit in new investments made with market-rate deposits. Thrifts, however, have recently lost money on their old investments, a result of another set of government regulations that will be reviewed in the next section of this chapter.

The falling away of rate controls has been bad news for thrift managers, as they anticipated. Although savings and loan associations and mutual savings banks are providing more deposit and lending services to the public than ever before, there is no longer a large cushion of below-market accounts to magnify profits and subsidize inefficient operations. The thrift industry is now going through a necessary restructuring that will lead to stronger, larger, leaner—but fewer—firms.

Despite the substantial decontrol that has taken place, the thrift industry continued to argue for retention of the remaining ceilings. Under a law passed in 1980, interest rate ceilings on deposits are required to be lifted by 1986.[13] The thrift industry called this a six-year extension of Regulation Q, while commercial banks saw it as the culmination of their efforts to end rate ceilings.[14] Every time substantial rate deregulation was attempted under the 1980 law, it was either challenged by thrift industry lawsuits or rescinded under pressure.[15] The thrift industry ultimately acquiesced to a major relaxation of rate controls late in 1982 in exchange for the removal of many regulatory restrictions and the authorization of government financial assistance to the industry.[16]

New Thrift Asset Powers

The depression-era financial regulations established savings and loan associations as specialists in mortgage finance. Laws, regulations, and the tax code compelled these firms to invest in long-term housing-related loans and prevented them from making short-term consumer or commercial loans. Nor could they offer checking accounts to their customers. Commercial banks, on the other hand, were permitted to do all of these things. Throughout the period of relative financial stability preceding the 1970s, both banks and thrifts were profitable in their respective investments. But in times of financial stress, banks have the flexibility to adapt while most savings associations do not. The problem is that thrifts must borrow short to lend long. By law and regulation, their liabilities are primarily short-term consumer deposits, whereas their assets are long-term fixed-rate mortgages. When interest rates rise, their average cost of funds adjusts to the new level much more quickly than the return on their asset portfolio. The lack of portfolio diversification at the thrift institutions has caused lower earnings compared with banks and has impaired their ability to serve the public. Figure 4–2 shows that the thrifts' net income as a percentage of average assets (the usual measure of profitability for financial corporations) has been much more volatile than the banks' over the past two decades and that profitability has been substantially lower for thrifts than for banks in the past few years.

Thrift institutions seek expanded asset powers to permit them to cope with the new financial environment. They want to be able to match the maturities of their assets to that of their liabilities by taking on shorter-term commercial and consumer loans. The deregulation of their principal liabilities—consumer deposits, described in the preceding section—is a major spur to asset deregulation, since rate ceilings were a means of holding down the cost of funds in line with the return on assets. Diversification of assets and liabilities is the market response to this problem of matching the yields and maturities of investments and borrowings.

Community banks constitute one group opposing thrift diversification. In many smaller communities across the country, only one or

FIGURE 4–2
Profit Cycles at Depository Institutions, 1961–1980

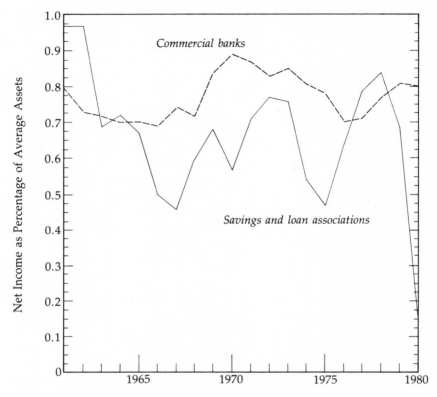

NOTES: Data are for retained earnings after all expenses, taxes, and dividends paid to depositors, as percentage of average assets. Data for commercial banks are for FDIC-insured institutions and since 1976 are based on consolidated reports. Data for savings and loan associations are for all associations since 1976 and FSLIC-insured institutions for prior years.

SOURCES: National Association of Mutual Savings Banks, *1982 National Fact Book of Savings Banking* (New York: NAMSB, 1982), p. 24.

two banks serve the deposit and lending needs of commercial and agricultural customers. The community banks do not today face direct competiton from the savings and loans already in place. These banks have an interest in denying expanded asset powers to thrift institutions, because it would mean the end of their monopoly.[17]

Bankers have not cast the debate in these terms, however. They have argued instead that the existing system has served the country well. The community bank industry states that thrifts can apply for bank charters if they wish bank powers, overlooking the restrictions on new bank charters imposed by many states and the other difficulties inherent in such a strategy. Further, they claim that blurring the distinction between banks and thrifts would hopelessly cloud antitrust enforcement. Banks and thrifts have been considered separate lines of commerce. When regulators assess the impact on market concentration of a proposed bank merger, they typically exclude thrifts from the relevant market. If thrifts are given banklike powers, it is feared, both sets of institutions will fall under the same market definition, reducing the measured level of concentration and allowing more bank mergers to take place than otherwise would be the case—leading ultimately to a massive concentration of power in the hands of big-city banks.

The issue has been contended between the representatives of the banking industry and those speaking for the thrifts. At issue, however, is the provision of a broad range of services demanded by borrowers and savers in an efficient manner and at competitive rates. Such a goal would be greatly served by an expansion of thrift asset powers, accompanied by whatever reforms are necessary to put banks on an equal footing.

The best example may be the state of Texas, where state-chartered savings and loan associations already have used many of the new asset powers. Thrifts there have proved to be formidable competitors of banks in meeting the financial needs of households and small businesses. Moreover, spurred by the competition, banks in Texas are now seeking the same liberal branching rules that now apply only to the savings and loan associations. The granting of such rules to banks will lead to even better access to financial services for consumers. The impetus for this further reform would not have existed without the expanded asset powers accorded thrifts in Texas.

The "housing industry" is a diverse collection of interests—home builders, real estate agents, construction workers, building supply firms, the lumber industry—but they have been united in their opposition to expanded asset powers for thrifts. Their concern is not over the new activities thrifts may enter but over the principal old area, housing, that they may leave.

Savings and loan associations began making long-term residential mortgage loans in the 1930s, when no other financial institutions were willing to do so. The government helped standardize the mortgage loan contract through the Federal Housing Administration, channeled funds from the national credit markets to housing through the Federal Home Loan Bank System, and demonstrated the role of secondary mortgage markets through establishment of the Federal National

Mortgage Association. For many years, the savings and loan associations were the principal instruments of housing growth, and they often had funds to lend when others did not.

The situation has now changed. As government programs demonstrated the viability of long-term mortgage lending, private industry moved in to assume many of the functions originally performed by government agencies. Yet the housing industry persists in the belief that without regulations compelling the thrifts to make housing loans, less mortgage finance will be available and interest rates will be higher. For example, those in the housing industry believe that commercial lending is inherently more profitable than mortgage lending and that home buyers would not be able to outbid corporations for scarce investment funds. The truth is that this competition for funds already exists because of the free flow of capital through the markets. The nominal interest rate on short-term business loans has been high in comparison with long-term mortgage rates at times during the past few years, but that is an anomalous situation affecting all classes of short- and long-term investments. Moreover, maturity differences aside, the greater costs and risks of many business loans demand higher rates so that the net risk-adjusted rate of return will match that of mortgage loans.

The housing interests also argue that thrifts perform a needed social function by making mortgage loans that a free market would not make. This may have been the case in the seriously distorted conditions of the 1930s, and it may have applied to some isolated markets as late as the 1960s, but it is certainly not true that thrifts subsidize mortgages today. In fact, in the last year, commercial banks have supplied more funds to the housing market than savings and loan associations—without the regulations and incentives that supposedly induce the thrifts.[18] The reasons that once may have existed for restricting savings and loan associations to housing investments have been largely demolished by the development and expansion of financial markets.

Limited new asset powers for the thrift industry were granted in the same 1980 act that provided for elimination of interest-rate controls on deposits. Substantial new authorities, including the all-important commercial lending powers, were debated and ultimately approved during the 1982 session of Congress. Even at that late date, the banking and housing interests were continuing to claim that more flexibility for thrifts was contrary to the public interest. Yet their private interests were clearly the major motivation. A spokesman for the community banking industry, when challenged, told a Senate committee chairman, "If I were the president of a savings and loan, my position would be just exactly the opposite of what it is. . . . That is just a person's vested interest of trying to get out of a difficult situation."[19] The housing industry views its troubles as flowing from a lack of mortgage money, an alleged problem that would be exacerbated by further moves to deregulate the savings and loan industry. Of course, the decline in real personal incomes, combined with high interest rates generally, explains the inability of many buyers to afford new houses.

The ability of the thrift industry to remain a viable competitor in the financial marketplace depends crucially on its ability to restructure and diversify. Thrifts can provide an alternative to commercial banks in many communities, spurring competition and efficiency.

Expanded Securities Powers for Banks

The Glass-Steagall Act of 1933 makes it unlawful for any firm engaged in the business of issuing, underwriting, selling, or distributing securities (investment banking) to engage in the business of deposit taking (commercial banking). There are two significant exceptions: commercial banks can deal in and underwrite general obligations of the federal, state, and municipal governments; and commercial banks can deal in securities for the accounts of their customers. Subsequent legislation (1968) permits commercial banks to underwrite housing, university, and dormitory revenue bonds as well as general obligation issues.

Within this framework, both commercial banks and investment banks have certain advantages and disadvantages, other than the obvious distinction between underwriting and deposit taking. Commercial banks are generally confined to operating within a single state, while securities firms may operate nationwide. Commercial banks can offer federal deposit insurance, whereas securities dealers cannot. Securities firms can form and sell mutual fund shares to the general public, including the versatile money market funds that some consumers use like bank accounts. And the rates on such money fund accounts are not controlled. Commercial banks can already operate all types of mutual funds for their trust accounts but not for their general customers.

The current debate revolves around two issues. Commercial banks want to round out their powers in the areas of municipal bond underwriting and selling mutual fund shares. Specifically, they seek authority to underwrite revenue bonds other than those involving housing, universities, or dormitories; and they want to be able to sell their mutual funds directly to the general public. These two points have been before Congress almost continuously for more than a decade.[20]

When the Glass-Steagall Act was passed, all municipal securities were general obligations—bonds backed by the full faith and credit of the issuing government unit—and commercial banks were permitted to participate fully in the underwriting process. Since that time, revenue bonds—issues backed by the expected income fom the investment project being financed—have gradually increased in importance. Revenue bonds now account for three-fourths of the annual $50 billion in new municipal issues.[21] Commercial banks have been a major element in the underwriting of general obligations, averaging about 40 percent of all such new issues. Banks' share of the total municipal market remains low, however, at about 20 percent, because they have been largely excluded from the growing revenue bond area.[22]

The commercial banks maintain that the increased competition they would bring to the revenue bond area would lower interest costs to issuers. Their efforts have been supported by the state and municipal governments who are the "consumers" in this case.[23] The banks are motivated not only by the prospect of profit opportunities, but also by the need to diversify as a result of the financial market deregulation described above.

Commercial banks are also seeking authority to form, operate, and sell mutual funds subject only to the regulations that now apply to securities firms. They are already permitted to do this for their trust accounts, so direct sale to the public is the issue. The industry maintains that the sale of mutual funds is a natural extension of its business.[24]

The securities industry has opposed both of these changes. These are areas that are now largely the exclusive preserves of the large regional and national broker–dealers. And securities firms already engage in many banklike activities, so they have a relatively advantageous position. Money market funds, for example, offer third-party payment capabilities, such as checks and credit cards. Some securities firms have also acquired interests in domestic and international banks.

Spokesmen for the securities industry dispute the banks' claims regarding savings to municipal issuers. There would also be the danger of a collapse in the financial system, they feel, if banks were to engage further in the "risky" business of underwriting. Rather than opening the revenue bond area to commercial banks, the securities industry has maintained that it would be more consistent with legislative intent to take away the banks' powers of the last fifty years to underwrite general obligation issues.[25]

With regard to mutual fund shares, the securities industry view is that banks are not sufficiently regulated for this activity to be conducted safely. It argues that conflicts of interest will arise from the mixing of financing and banking activities. For example, a bank might be tempted to use its knowledge of a loan customer's transactions to make investment decisions with respect to that company's stock.[26]

The securities industry's objections overlook the fact that banks have conducted essentially similar activities for many years with no apparent ill effects. There are also two strong incentives for banks to continue conducting such activities in a prudent manner. In the first place, banks are shareholder-owned institutions with an interest in operating safely and profitably over the long term. And second, it is possible to correct the deficiencies alleged by the securities industry simply by extending existing securities regulations to banks; it is not necessary to deny banks the opportunity of engaging in the activities.

In fact, bank entry into these two areas of the securities industry would make more services available to bank customers. Increased competition between commercial banks and investment banks would promote efficiency and possibly reduce the underwriting expense on revenue bonds. Revenue bond and mutual fund authority were proposed in legislation debated by Congress in 1982, and once again the opposition used the arguments described here to defeat the reforms.

Conclusion

The existing regulatory structure served the country and its financial system well for most of the past fifty years. But conditions have changed, and regulation must adapt. Agreement on needed modification is often difficult to achieve, however, as the discussion here has shown. The regulations originally intended to promote the safety and soundness of the financial system have come to serve purely private interests as well. This has motivated opposition to reform and efforts to retain existing preferences. Forces opposing the reforms have often been successful due to a lack of organized public support for change.

Notes

1. For a general discussion of this issue, see Patric H. Hendershott, "Deregulation and the Capital Markets: The Impact of Deposit Rate Ceilings and Restrictions Against Variable Rate Mortgages," in Lawrence G. Goldberg and Lawrence J. White, eds., *The Deregulation of the Banking and Securities Industries* (Lexington, Mass.: Lexington Books, 1979), pp. 71–100.

2. See Robert A. Taggart, Jr., "Effects of Deposit Rate Ceilings," *Journal of Money, Credit, and Banking,* vol. 10 (May 1978), pp. 139–57; and Robert A. Taggart and Geoffrey Woglom, "Savings Bank Reactions to Rate Ceilings and Rising Market Rates," *New England Economic Review* (Federal Reserve Bank of Boston, September/October 1978), pp. 17–31.

3. Comparison of 1961–1967 with 1967–1978. U.S. League of Savings Associations, *'81 Savings and Loan Sourcebook* (Chicago, Ill.: USLSA, 1982), pp. 37, 40; and previous issues.

4. Patric H. Hendershott and Kevin E. Villani, *Regulation and Reform of the Housing Finance System* (Washington, D.C.: American Enterprise Institute, 1978); Donald Hester, "Special Interests: The FINE Solution," *Journal of Money, Credit, and Banking*, vol. 9 (November 1977), pp. 652–61.

5. Edward J. Kane, "Getting Along Without Regulation Q: Testing the Standard View of Deposit Rate Competition during the 'Wild-Card Experience,' " *Journal of Finance*, vol. 33 (June 1978), pp. 921–32; Almarin Phillips, "Competitive Policy for Depository Financial Institutions," in Almarin Phillips, ed., *Promoting Competition in Regulated Markets* (Washington, D.C.: Brookings Institution, 1975), pp. 329–66.

6. Charles Clotfelter and Charles Lieberman, "On the Distributional Impact of Federal Interest Rate Restrictions," *Journal of Finance*, vol. 33 (March 1978), pp. 199–213; David H. Pyle, "The Losses on Savings Deposits from Interest Rate Regulation," *Bell Journal of Economics and Management Science*, vol. 5 (Autumn 1974), pp. 614–22.

7. See Andrew S. Carron, *The Plight of the Thrift Institutions* (Washington, D.C.: Brookings Institution, 1982), pp. 61–65; and *The Report of the President's Commission on Housing*, 1982, pp. 124–27.

8. Carron, *Plight of the Thrift Institutions*, p. 9.

9. Ibid., pp. 18–19.

10. Federal Home Loan Bank Board (FHLBB), news release, October 12, 1982; USLSA, *'81 Sourcebook*, p. 19.

11. See sources for figure 4–1.

12. FHLBB, unpublished data, 1982.

13. Title II of the Depository Institutions Deregulation and Monetary Control Act of 1980, 94 Stat. 143.

14. See the statement of Edwin B. Brooks, Jr., president, U.S. League of Savings Associations, in *Depository Institutions Deregulation Committee, Hearings before the Senate Committee on Banking, Housing, and Urban Affairs*, 96th Cong., 2d sess., 1980, p. 63.

15. Carron, *Plight of the Thrift Institutions*, pp. 56–58.

16. Garn–St Germain Depository Institutions Act of 1982, Public Law 97-320, 96 Stat. 1469.

17. Stephen A. Rhoades, "Welfare Loss, Redistribution Effect, and Restriction of Output Due to Monopoly in Banking," *Journal of Monetary Economics*, vol. 9 (May 1982), pp. 375–87; Phillips, "Competitive Policy," in Phillips, ed., *Promoting Competition*.

18. Board of Governors of the Federal Reserve System, *Flow of Funds Accounts, Second Quarter 1982* (September 1982), p. 37.

19. Statement of Robert L. McCormick, Jr., president, Independent Bankers Association of America, in *Capital Assistance Act and Deposit Insurance Flexibility Act, Hearings before the Senate Committee on Banking, Housing, and Urban Affairs*, 97th Cong., 2d sess., 1982, p. 375.

20. See Lee A. Pickard, "A Need for Change in Direction in Regulation of the Securities Markets," in Goldberg and White, eds., *Deregulation of the Banking and Securities Industries*, pp. 63–70; Franklin R. Edwards, "Banks and Securities Activities: Legal and Economic Perspectives on the Glass-Steagall Act," in ibid., pp. 273–94; James W. Stevens, "The Intersection of the Banking and Securities Industries and Future Deregulation," in ibid., pp. 295–304; Harvey A. Rowen, "The Intersection of the Banking and Securities Industries and Future Deregulation," in ibid., pp. 305–22; and David L. Ratner, "Deregulation of the Intersection of the Banking and Securities Industries," in ibid., pp. 323–34.

21. Public Securities Association, unpublished data, 1981.

22. Securities and Exchange Commission, Directorate of Economic and Policy Re-

search, *Bank Participation in Municipal Bond Underwriting: Impact on Securities Industry Revenues*, 1979.

23. Reuben Kessel, "A Study of the Effects of Competition in the Tax-exempt Bond Market," *Journal of Political Economy*, vol. 79 (July/August 1971), pp. 706–38; Phillip Cagan, "The Interest Saving to States and Municipalities from Bank Eligibility to Underwrite All Nonindustrial Municipal Bonds," *Governmental Finance*, vol. 7 (May 1978), pp. 40–48.

24. Phillips, "Competitive Policy," in Phillips, ed., *Promoting Competition*.

25. Securities Industry Association, "Bank Securities Activities: Memorandum for Study and Discussion," *San Diego Law Review*, vol. 14 (June 1977), pp. 751-822.

26. Ibid.

5

Air Pollution, Environmentalists, and the Coal Lobby

ROBERT W. CRANDALL

The control of sulfur-oxides emissions is a very important component of federal and state air pollution policies. Airborne sulfur dioxide (SO_2) is probably harmful to human health and vegetation, but it appears that its most serious threat is to human health after it has been transformed into sulfates in the atmosphere.[1] These sulfates are deposited in the form of "acid rain," damaging streams, lakes, and wildlife. As the knowledge about the potential damage from airborne sulfates has developed, environmental authorities and the congressional committees responsible for environmental issues have looked for better mechanisms to reduce sulfur emissions.

In 1975, Congress began the search for a new sulfur-oxides policy. It was concerned that sulfur-oxides and particulates emissions would increase in the less populous but growing areas of the country, thereby degrading presently clean, healthy air. Moreover, it feared that the switch to coal would increase emissions everywhere, particularly in the populous industrial Midwest. Its solution to both of these problems in the 1977 Clean Air Act amendments reflected a curious mixture of interest-group politics that carried over into the administrative process of the Environmental Protection Agency (EPA) in 1978–1979.[2] The result of this political coalition-building has been an unnecessarily expensive, growth-inhibiting set of standards that confers only minor benefits upon some constituent groups and contributes very little to general environmental quality.

Coal and the Sulfur-Oxides Problem

Eighty percent of sulfur-oxides emissions result from the burning of oil or coal.[3] Throughout the 1960s, the average level of airborne SO_2 appeared to decline as a result of state and local government pressures

84

on electric utilities. Oil was substituted for coal, and low-sulfur fuels were required in many areas. Flue-gas desulfurization systems (scrubbers) were developed, but they were thought to be unreliable and were very expensive. Utilities such as American Electric Power resisted using scrubbers, arguing that other technologies for limiting sulfur emissions were more efficient.

After the Arab oil embargo in the autumn of 1973, the price of oil rose very rapidly. The high price of oil began to stimulate a return to the use of coal in electric utilities. Environmentalists were worried that the shift back to coal-fired plants would be very damaging to national air quality.

Fortunately, the United States has large deposits of low-sulfur coal near the surface in western states such as Montana, Wyoming, and Colorado. Eighty percent of the low-sulfur coal reserves of the United States are west of the Mississippi.[4] This low-sulfur coal, although expensive to transport to the populous consuming regions, could be burned with relatively little discharge of SO_2 and more cheaply than oil in many regions. The development of the western coal reserves, however, was viewed as a threat to the eastern and midwestern coal industry, whose deposits are generally higher in sulfur and more expensive to mine. Most of this disparity in costs derives from the depth and width of the seams and the lower productivity of labor that results from such geological differences. As a result, even surface-mined eastern or midwestern coal is generally more costly at the minehead than coal from Montana or Wyoming.

While low-sulfur western coal might be the answer to the search for a clean, low-cost fuel in a world of soaring energy prices, it began to look threatening to the owners, operators, and employees of many coal mines in the Midwest and the East. Environmentalists were alarmed by the idea of giant strip-mining operations on the western plateau. Moreover, they thought, the development of this low-sulfur coal might delay the development of pollution-control devices—such as stack-gas scrubbers—which were so important to them.

The 1977 Clean Air Act Amendments

In 1975, Congress began to search for new ways to control sulfur oxides. The rush toward coal would soon reverse the progress of the 1960s in improving SO_2 concentrations around the country. And much of the increase in the use of coal would come in areas with relatively clean air. How could this problem be addressed in a politically palatable way?

At the time, relatively few areas of the country had health-endangering concentrations of sulfur oxides. While scientists were beginning to worry about the effects of certain sulfate compounds and their deposition as acid rain, SO_2 was not a serious *local* problem in most areas. It was therefore difficult to induce the states to place tighter limits on existing SO_2 sources, which are principally electric utilities. On the other hand, *new* industry and utility installations could be saddled with tighter controls.

In 1971, EPA had set the standard for new plants—the new source performance standard—at 1.2 pounds of SO_2 per million B.t.u.s. This standard had to be met by all new sources regardless of local air quality or the sulfur content of the fuel. Congress could have legislated a tighter new-source standard in 1977, but there was apparently very little political support for it. While it might lower sulfur-oxides emissions in future years, the effect would be so gradual that few voters would even perceive it. Utilities would be opposed, of course, and might even sway the average voter with arguments about future electricity costs. Eastern and midwestern coal producers and their employees would be vehemently opposed because tighter new-source standards would reduce the demand for their dirty coal.

The House Environmental Subcommittee staff began to look for some mechanism to force reduction in future sulfur-oxides emissions that could command widespread political support.[5] Their first choice was a new provision in section 111 of the Clean Air Act that would require new coal-burning facilities to utilize "the best technological system of continuous emission reduction" regardless of the quality of the fuel. This was understood to mean that expensive stack-gas scrubbers were to be used on all new industrial and utility sources regardless of the sulfur content of the fuel burned. The requirement would reduce the incentive for utilities to import low-sulfur western coal, since high-sulfur local coal would be cheaper in most locations. In the West and Southwest, where low-sulfur coal is plentiful, the scrubbing requirement would have less effect upon emissions, but it would add just as much to the cost of each new coal-fired installation.

The impact of this proposal, which eventually became part of the 1977 Clean Air Act amendments, is best explained with an example. Assume that an electric utility wishes to build a new coal-fired plant in Illinois. It could buy cheap local coal that produces perhaps 10 pounds of SO_2 per million B.t.u.s, or it could import much more expensive coal from Wyoming that yields only 1 pound of SO_2 per million B.t.u.s. If the performance standard were 1 pound of SO_2 per million B.t.u.s and if a scrubber could remove 90 percent of SO_2, the utility would weigh the cost differences between the two coal sources against the cost of buying and operating a scrubber, which could add as much as 20 percent to the cost of a new power plant. If the western coal has less of a premium per million B.t.u.s than the cost of owning and operating a scrubber, it would buy western coal.

With the amendment to section 111, the utility would have no choice. If a scrubber were required, the utility would always opt for the coal that produces 10 pounds of SO_2 per million B.t.u.s. In fact, under the final EPA rule, it might choose even dirtier local coal with 12 pounds of SO_2 per million B.t.u.s. Even if 0.5 pound (of SO_2) western coal were available at a modest premium, the utility would have no incentive to use it. It would choose the dirtiest and cheapest coal available.

Obviously this forcing of scrubbers is neither good economic policy nor good environmental policy. Coal users have no incentive to use the most efficient methods for limiting their SO_2 emissions, nor do they have an incentive to choose the least polluting combination of fuel and technology.

Surprisingly, the environmentalists fell in behind the House subcommittee proposal. Perhaps they felt that this was a reasonable method for "forcing" technology on recalcitrant utilities. It is a fundamental belief of most environmental lobbyists that Congress must force technology by requiring the "best available" emissions abatement techniques to be used on new facilities. This, they believe, will stimulate equipment producers to look for better control technologies regardless of their cost.

Perhaps the environmentalists thought that once the scrubbers were installed, they could argue for ever tighter performance standards or for a "ceiling" upon emissions. For instance, they could use the rule-making process to press for maximum emissions of 0.6 pound per million B.t.u.s, thereby forbidding the use of coal with more than 6 pounds of SO_2 per million B.t.u.s. But unless they were successful in obtaining this low ceiling on emissions in conjunction with the scrubbing requirements, the environmentalists would risk increasing the emissions level in certain areas where high-sulfur coal is plentiful.

It is not surprising that the eastern and midwestern coal producers and the United Mine Workers joined the environmentalists and the subcommittee staff in support of mandatory scrubbing. The United Mine Workers (UMW) are heavily represented in eastern coal districts but have not succeeded in organizing most of the western industry. This clean air/dirty coal lobby was then joined by the Carter administration, which supported the proposal as a means of saving jobs in Appalachia and the Midwest.[6]

There was little effective western or southwestern opposition to the new section 111, despite the fact that it would raise the costs of electric power in these more rapidly growing areas far more than necessary to preserve clean air. These regions have billions of tons of low-sulfur coal in their backyards that they could have burned relatively cleanly, but they, too, would be required to install expensive stack-gas scrubbers.

The Coal Market

Given the central role of the eastern coal industry and the UMW in the environmental issue it is useful to describe the situation in the coal industry in the mid-1970s and the prospects for it under alternative environmental rules. Coal had been a stagnant industry from 1950 through the 1970s because of the nation's concern about air quality. With declining real prices of oil and increasing state and local concern over air quality, utilities were switching from coal to oil. Coal production had grown only from 560 million tons in 1950 to 610 million tons in 1974, and the eastern and midwestern industries had borne much of the costs of this stagnation.[7]

With the rapid escalation in oil prices in 1973–1974, however, the future of coal began to look promising once again. Coal was the low-cost fuel for new utility plants in much of the country, and the federal government was even empowered to mandate some conversions from oil or natural gas to coal. The existence of vast low-cost deposits of low-sulfur coal in the western states offered the promise of a great expansion of coal burning without an intolerable increase in SO_2 emissions.

How would the Appalachian and midwestern coal industries fare in this new world of high oil prices and heightened environmental concern? Surprisingly, forecasts made before, during, and after EPA's setting of the final scrubber rule did not indicate a major decline in coal production in these high-sulfur coal areas. Forecasts made by ICF, Inc., a Washington, D.C., consulting firm, for EPA in 1976, 1978, and 1979 and a recent forecast made by the Congressional Budget Office (CBO) are shown in table 5–1.

In 1976, EPA was predicting a 40 percent increase in eastern coal production between 1975 and 1990 without any change in EPA standards. Midwestern coal was projected to decline by 17 percent in this period, hardly a precipitous decline. Overall, eastern and midwestern coal were projected to *increase* by 24 percent in this fifteen-year period even if the Congress did not amend the Clean Air Act.

By August 1978, even these forecasts were appearing far too pessimistic. It is perhaps not surprising that once EPA immersed itself in the rule making to respond to the congressional revision of section

TABLE 5-1

COAL PRODUCTION: ACTUAL 1975 OUTPUT VERSUS PREDICTIONS FOR
1990, 1995, AND 2000 WITH 1971 NEW-SOURCE STANDARDS

	Production Year	Region		
		East	Midwest	West
Actual	1975	396 (61%)	151 (23%)	100 (15%)
EPA predictions				
February 1976	1990	555 (41%)	125 (9%)	686 (50%)
August 1978	1990	465 (30%)	275 (18%)	785 (51%)
June 1979	1995	489 (27%)	404 (23%)	885 (50%)
CBO prediction				
April 1982	2000	696 (38%)	250 (14%)	897 (49%)

NOTE: Figures are millions of tons per year; percentage of national total.
SOURCES: U.S. Environmental Protection Agency, "A Preliminary Analysis of the Economic Impact of Alternative Approaches to Significant Deterioration," February 5, 1976; USEPA, *Electric Utility Steam Generating Units: Background Information for Proposed SO_2 Emission Standards*, August 1978; and USEPA, "New Stationary Sources Performance Standards; Electric Utility Steam Generating Units," *Federal Register*, vol. 44, no. 113 (June 11, 1979); Congressional Budget Office, *The Clean Air Act, the Electric Utilities, and the Coal Market*, April 1982.

111, it found that even the midwestern coal industry would not have declined in the face of the old standard. Now EPA was predicting that midwestern coal would have risen by 82 percent between 1975 and 1990 without congressional intervention. Eastern coal, on the other hand, would have increased in production by only 17 percent.

Four years later, the Congressional Budget Office prepared a study showing that both eastern and midwestern coal production would have increased substantially by the year 2000 even if the Congress had not revised the new source standard. Eastern production, according to CBO, would have increased to 696 million tons, or 76 percent from its 1975 level. Midwestern coal would have expanded by 66 percent, a startling growth rate for a coal region dominated by high-sulfur deposits. These projections do not have the ring of crisis that would require an emasculation of the Clean Air Act.

There has been little doubt that western coal production would increase in the next two decades. The EPA and CBO analyses have consistently shown substantial growth in western coal production through 1990 or 2000 with the old new-source standard. The 1976 EPA projection for western coal in 1990 was 686 million tons, or a six-fold increase over 1974. By 1978, this forecast had grown to 785 million tons. In 1982, the CBO forecast western production at 897 million tons by the year 2000, assuming no change in the 1971 new-source performance standard.

By 1976, it was clear, therefore, that the high price of oil and the concern over air pollution would radically shift the future production of coal from eastern and midwestern regions to the West—principally the northern Great Plains. *But this did not mean that the eastern regions would suffer a decline in output, only that they would not grow as rapidly as their western brethren.* Clean coal would increasingly be transported from the West to midwestern consuming regions. Surely, this is a result that environmentalists should have applauded. Clean resources were going to substitute for dirtier resources.

The Effects of Scrubbing on Coal Production

If coal production was shifting westward because of the lower sulfur content of western deposits, would requiring scrubbers on all new industrial or utility boilers reverse or stop this trend? As it turns out, there is apparently at best a very small shift in the geographical distribution of coal production under various regulatory approaches. Even assuming a full scrubbing standard (which EPA did not adopt), the shift from western to eastern production is very small. In 1976, EPA forecast that full scrubbing would increase coal production in the eastern and midwestern regions by only 33 million tons, or 4.9 percent, by 1990 (table 5–2). Western coal production would be reduced by 4.7 percent (32 million tons) according to this analysis. By 1978, EPA had reduced its estimate of the benefits to eastern and midwestern producers to 3.6 percent, but the reduction in western output by 1990 was now forecast to be 6.2 percent.[8]

The 1982 CBO study saw even smaller benefits to eastern and midwestern coal producers from EPA's final new-source standard. This standard required less sulfur removal from the stack gases of low-sulfur coal and is therefore not fully comparable with the full-scrubbing analyses done by EPA in 1976 and 1978. CBO shows that the new EPA standards actually *increase* western coal production by less than 1 percent by the year 2000, increase midwestern coal production by only 7.6 percent, and leave eastern coal output virtually unchanged.[9] The increase in "western" coal occurs mostly in the Gulf states (Texas and Louisiana). The effect of the final scrubbing rule is to reduce Great Plains coal production by 26 million tons (5.7 percent) by the year 2000. These changes are so small that one wonders why so much political effort was expended on the issue.

TABLE 5–2

CHANGES IN ANNUAL COAL PRODUCTION DUE TO
IMPOSITION OF STACK-GAS SCRUBBING

Date of Prediction	Production Year	Region		
		East	Midwest	West
EPA				
February 1976	1990	+ 9 (+1.6%)	+24 (+19.2%)	−32 (−4.7%)
August 1978[a]	1990	−16 (−3.4%)	+43 (+15.6%)	−49 (−6.2%)
June 1979[b]	1995	−26 (−5.3%)	+83 (+20.5%)	−70 (−7.9%)
CBO				
April 1982[b]	2000	− 2 (−0.3%)	+19 (+ 7.6%)	+ 7 (+0.8%)

NOTE: Figures are millions of tons per year; percentage of national total.
a. Assumes 0.2 lb./million B.t.u. floor and 1.2 lb./million B.t.u. ceiling.
b. Effect of current rule (70 percent and 90 percent removal).
SOURCE: Same as for table 5-1.

The EPA Rule Making

EPA's final scrubbing rule has been roundly criticized by Ackerman and Hassler, who contend that the agency should have looked for other alternatives in view of its responsibilities under the Clean Air Act. EPA's final decision was to require 90 percent scrubbing for all high-sulfur coal and 70 percent scrubbing for very low sulfur coal. This was a small concession to rationality, since the 70 percent requirement is obviously less expensive than 90 percent scrubbing.[10] Even so, the standard imposes considerable costs upon those seeking to burn low-sulfur coal, and it will induce many utilities to buy higher-sulfur coal if they must pay for a scrubber anyway.

EPA accepted evidence that scrubbers *can* remove as much as 90 percent of SO_2 from stack gases when operating efficiently, but it ignored the fact that it has neither the technology nor the resources to assure compliance with the SO_2 emissions limits from new or old plants. Stack-gas scrubbers require enormous amounts of maintenance, which utilities are unlikely to provide in a diligent manner if environmental authorities do not monitor their results carefully. When 10-pound coal is being burned, a scrubber failure can lead to enormous increases in emissions. The burning of low-sulfur coal carries no such risks. Therefore, it is possible that full SO_2 scrubbing increases costs and emissions concurrently—hardly the result an environmental policy maker would wish.

Given the costs that the scrubbing standard imposes and the perverse results it could engender, why did EPA not consider other technologies, such as the pretreatment of relatively low sulfur coal? It apparently read its mandate narrowly because of intense pressure from environmentalists and the eastern coal lobby. Environmentalists wanted an even tighter standard of 95 percent scrubbing, and they even sued EPA for failing to be sufficiently irrational.[11] This suit failed.

The coal lobby worked very hard through the nearly two years of rule making to ensure that the final result would allow new plants to burn dirty coal. The lobbyists finally gained access to the White House and EPA in the last month of the process, a triumph that culminated in two meetings during which the Senate majority leader (from West Virginia) argued strenuously for a rule that would require scrubbing but would allow maximum emissions of 1.2 pounds per million B.t.u.s.[12] This stricture would allow very high sulfur coal from the Midwest and Appalachia to be used in new plants. In the last two weeks, EPA caved in to this pressure, abandoning its earlier advocacy of a ceiling between 0.55 and 0.80 pounds per million B.t.u.s. The coal lobby had thus succeeded in using the environmentalists to force EPA to allow extremely high sulfur coal to be burned. Utilities would be required to install costly scrubbers, but they would not be required to lower their maximum emissions from new plants. Costs would rise and air quality would suffer as a result.

The Effect on Air Quality

If the effect of requiring expensive stack-gas scrubbers on coal production is small, the effect upon emissions is equally modest. EPA projections of the reductions in emissions from scrubbing have never been very large. In its 1976 study, EPA projected sizable reductions in emissions due to a combination of regulatory changes involving nondeterioration and New-Source Performance Standards (NSPS). The full-scrubbing requirement by itself was estimated to reduce SO_2 emissions from 15.6 million tons per year to 12.1 million tons by 1990.[13]

This reduction was found to be substantially overoptimistic by 1978, when EPA faced the real choices on scrubbing. Whereas the earlier study had forecast substantial emissions *reductions* from 1974 to 1990, EPA was now conceding that under any of its choices of scrubbing rules, emissions from utility boilers would increase. By 1995, if the old NSPS rule were in force, utility plant emissions would rise from their level of 18.6 million tons in 1975 to 23.8 million tons of SO_2. A full-scrubbing requirement would reduce this to 20.7 million tons, or by 13 percent.[14] This analysis assumed that scrubbers would work to their theoretical potential and that EPA would be able to enforce the standard. Given very poor EPA enforcement capabilities and the frequent malfunctioning of scrubbers, this estimate must be considered exceedingly optimistic.

What is more surprising, however, is the impact of the final, less onerous, variable-scrubbing rule, requiring only 70 percent removal of SO_2 from low-sulfur coal. Under this variable-scrubbing rule, control costs are lower, and emissions are estimated to be 20.5 million tons in 1990, or 0.2 million tons less than from the stricter, full-scrubbing, rule.[15] The reason for lower emissions and costs is the expense imposed by the stricter rule, which induces utilities to postpone replacement of older, dirty plants with the new, cleaner ones. Despite this result, environmentalists generally pressed for the full-scrubbing alternative, and some even wanted a stronger, 95 percent, full-scrubbing requirement that would have yielded even greater postponements and higher emissions rates through 1995.

The regional distribution of emissions provides an equally interesting story. The acid deposition problem is greatest in the Midwest and the East, and it is generally believed that the increasing acidity of lakes in the East is due at least in part to midwestern SO_2 emissions. Moreover, most of the SO_2 emissions from electric utilities are generated in the East and the Midwest.

The scrubbing requirement succeeds in lowering emissions modestly as we have seen (assuming that the scrubbers work precisely to specification), but a very large share of this reduction occurs in the West and Southwest, where emissions are already low. Table 5–3 reproduces EPA analyses, which indicated that emissions in the West and West South Central regions of the country will be reduced from 4.3 million tons to 2.8 million tons per year by 1995 with the imposition of the EPA scrubbing rules. The East and the Midwest, on the other hand, have their emissions reduced only from 19.5 million tons to 17.7 million tons per year by 1995.[16] Thus, the scrubbing rule reduces western and southwestern emissions by more than a third while reducing eastern and midwestern SO_2 by only 9 percent, despite the fact that the latter are nearly five times the former. In short, the new rule does very little to improve air quality in those areas that have the biggest problem while imposing very large emissions-reduction burdens upon the growing western and southwestern portions of the country.

TABLE 5–3

PREDICTED SO$_2$ EMISSIONS IN 1995 UNDER ALTERNATIVE
NEW-SOURCE RULES FOR ELECTRIC UTILITIES
(millions of tons per year)

	1975 Actual	Old Standards	Full Scrubbing (90% removal)	Final EPA Rule (70% to 90% removal)
National	18.6	23.8	20.7	20.5
Regional				
East		11.2	10.1	9.7
Midwest		8.3	7.9	8.0
West South				
Central		2.6	1.7	1.7
West		1.7	0.9	1.1

SOURCE: U.S. Environmental Protection Agency, "New Stationary Sources Performance Standards; Electric Utility Steam Generating Units," *Federal Register*, vol. 44, no. 113 (June 11, 1979).

The Effect on Costs

Given the modest impact of the new scrubbing rules for SO$_2$ emissions on air quality and the distribution of coal production, the new rules are surprisingly expensive. According to EPA's analyses, the cost of the rule that it finally chose—90 percent reduction for high-sulfur coal and 70 percent reduction for low-sulfur coal—is $3.3 billion per year by 1995.[17] This translates into a cost per ton of SO$_2$ removal of between $1,000 and $1,200, assuming that the flue-gas scrubbers operate to theoretical expectations. If these scrubbers are not maintained adequately or do not perform up to expectations, the cost per ton could be considerably higher. And this estimate fails to capture the very high costs of sulfur-oxides control for users of low-sulfur coal. The EPA analysis admits that these costs are between $1,700 and $2,000 per ton removed, far above the costs of control for other sources of SO$_2$.[18]

If EPA were to revert to the old performance standard of 1.2 pounds per million B.t.u.s, it could save utilities $3.3 billion per year by 1995 according to the EPA analysis. EPA projected that this older standard would increase emissions by 3.3 million tons by 1995. According to a more recent CBO analysis, the effect of reverting to the old standards would be an increase of only 1.8 million tons in annual SO_2 emissions by 2000 but a savings of $4.34 billion (1980 dollars) per year by that time. Thus, CBO estimates that the cost of the scrubbing standard is about $2,400 per ton of SO_2 abated by 2000.[19]

A simple performance standard, limiting all new source emissions to perhaps 1.0 pounds per million B.t.u.s would be much less costly and as effective in reducing SO_2. The CBO analysis demonstrates that a policy designed to equate marginal control costs at new and old sources could achieve the same emissions results as EPA's final rule at annual savings of $3.35 billion by 2000.

The Political Appeal of the Scrubbing Requirement

Given the dismal facts of the situation, why does scrubbing have such continuing appeal to congressmen? There cannot be enough congressional districts with high-sulfur coal mining to produce a strong vote for this heroically inefficient approach. Yet the current Congress refuses to tamper with the scrubbing requirement.

The appeal of the scrubbing rule obviously extends beyond the dirty-coal districts. Most of the effect of the requirement is borne by the western and southwestern states. Having cheap low-sulfur coal, these states could build and operate new power plants more efficiently than their eastern and midwestern counterparts. Requiring even 70 percent removal of SO_2 from stack gases already low in sulfur greatly increases western and southwestern utility costs. In fact, EPA found that full (90 percent) scrubbing would raise southwestern utility prices by as much as 11 percent in a decade but those in the Midwest and East by less than 2 percent.[20] With industry already fleeing the industrial Midwest and East for the Sun Belt, this "environmental" policy change could serve as at least a partial barrier to further migration. For this reason, industrial lobbies have been curiously silent on the scrubbing issue in the most recent round of testimony on reauthorization of the Clean Air Act. The Reagan administration favors repeal of the rule, but it has found very little support for its position.

Notes

1. Lester B. Lave and Eugene P. Seskin, *Air Pollution and Human Health*, Resources for the Future Series (Baltimore: The Johns Hopkins University Press, 1977).

2. For a description of this political battle, see Bruce A. Ackerman and William T. Hassler, *Clean Coal/Dirty Air: Or How the Clean Air Act Became a Multibillion-Dollar Bail-Out for High-Sulfur Coal Producers and What Should Be Done about It* (New Haven: Yale University Press, 1981).

3. U.S. Environmental Protection Agency, *National Air Pollutant Emissions Estimates, 1940–80,* EPA-450/4-82-001, January 1982.

4. U.S. Environmental Protection Agency, *Electric Utility Steam Generating Units: Background Information for Proposed SO$_2$ Emission Standards,* EPA-450/2-78-007a, July 1978.

5. Ackerman and Hassler, *Clean Coal/Dirty Air,* pp. 27-33.

6. Testimony of Douglas Costle, EPA administrator, in *Clean Air Act Amendments of 1977, Hearings before the Subcommittee on Health and the Environment of the House Committee on Interstate and Foreign Commerce,* 95th Cong., 1st sess., 1977, pp. 1684-85.

7. U.S. Bureau of Mines, *Mineral Yearbook,* 1976.

8. U.S. Environmental Protection Agency, *Electric Utility Steam Generating Units: Background Information for Proposed SO$_2$ Emission Standards,* August 1978.

9. Congressional Budget Office, *The Clean Air Act, the Electric Utilities, and the Coal Market,* April 1982.

10. For a discussion of EPA's final decision, see Ackerman and Hassler, *Clean Coal/ Dirty Air,* and U.S. Environmental Protection Agency, "New Stationary Sources Performance Standards; Electric Utility Steam Generating Units," *Federal Register,* vol. 44, no. 113 (June 11, 1979).

11. Sierra Club v. Costle, 657 F.2d 298 (D.C. Cir. 1981).

12. Ackerman and Hassler, *Clean Coal/Dirty Air,* p. 100.

13. U.S. Environmental Protection Agency, "A Preliminary Analysis."

14. U.S. Environmental Protection Agency, "New Stationary Sources Performance Standards."

15. Ibid.

16. Ibid.

17. Ibid.

18. Ibid.

19. Congressional Budget Office, *The Clean Air Act.*

20. U.S. Environmental Protection Agency, *Electric Utility Steam Generating Units.*

6

The Creation, Growth, and Entrenchment of Special Interests in Oil Price Policy

JOSEPH P. KALT

The early 1970s marked a watershed in U.S. energy policy. For reasons largely beyond the nation's control, energy prices throughout the world took off on a rise that would not stop. The country was put under tremendous pressure to adapt an economy that had been nurtured on relatively cheap and abundant liquid fuels to the sudden reality of markedly increased energy scarcity. At stake were short-term and long-term national economic growth, the demand for and productivity of labor, international competitiveness, and even the position of the United States in the global political arena.

By all accounts, the nation has not performed well in the face of the challenge presented to it by the energy crisis. A principal, if not dominant, source of this failure has been federal energy regulatory policy. This policy has consistently forestalled the adjustment by both energy producers and energy consumers to a world of higher prices. In countless examples, this has been the result of originally well-intentioned temporary measures designed to soften the blow of reality on individuals deemed to be deserving. Yet, the repeated consequence has been the creation and solidification of vested interests ultimately unwilling to relinquish their access to regulatory largess.

A review of oil price regulation provides an especially clear illustration of narrowly conceived, but ultimately far-reaching and long-living, energy policies. Originally adopted as a part of a 90-day economy-wide emergency measure to stop a rise in inflation in 1971, oil price controls were eventually embodied in well-targeted legislation designed to deal with the emergency of the Arab oil embargo in the winter of 1973–1974. These "temporary" controls far outlived the emergencies that gave them birth and lasted just six and one-half months short of a full decade. Over this period, the nation's petroleum markets were subjected to no fewer than six different regulatory agencies and seven distinct price control regimes, each successively more complicated and pervasive. Indeed, even the ending of oil price controls in January 1981 appears to have been a change more of form than of substance, as many of the central economic tenets of controls are now embodied in a multilayered system of federal excise taxes scheduled to last into the 1990s.[1]

During the near decade of regulation, economists and other policy analysts of all political persuasions reached virtually unanimous agreement that the system was extremely deleterious to the U.S. economy.[2] Moreover, each of the last three presidents pursued policies of decontrol. Why, then, were oil price controls so difficult for the political decision-making system to jettison?

The answer is found in a pattern that is much closer to the rule than the exception in regulatory histories: regulations adopted to address a specific and fairly well defined problem create unintended economic distortions. These resulting problems are addressed with further stop-gap regulations. The cycle repeats itself; and at each stage there are economic winners and losers as regulation alters prices, costs, contracts, supplies, and demands. Affected parties that are well organized and well endowed financially are coalesced and inevitably influence the growing patchwork of regulation. The end result is a system that, in its overall design, accords with no one's conception of sound economic policy for the country but has a well-entrenched special interest residing in each of its component parts.

Background on Policy

On August 15, 1971, President Nixon imposed a three-month freeze on virtually all wages and prices, including oil prices, in the United States. This freeze became known as Phase I of the Nixon administration's anti-inflation program. This program went through a number of phases over several years, with petroleum markets successively singled out for more and more special treatment. By late summer of 1973, most of the economy had been substantially freed from wage and price controls, whereas detailed and stringent price regulations were promulgated for the petroleum sector. Within weeks after the start of the Arab oil embargo in October 1973, these regulations were embodied in the Emergency Petroleum Allocation Act of 1973 (EPAA; Public Law 93–159). Originally scheduled to expire in February 1975, the oil pricing provisions of EPAA were amended and extended numerous times and did not officially expire until September 30, 1981.

EPAA controlled the prices of both crude oil and refined petroleum products. Initially, the act categorized crude oil prices into two tiers—one controlled and one uncontrolled. The controlled tier covered so-called old oil from properties brought into production prior to 1973. Uncontrolled oil included oil from new properties, any production from older properties in excess of pre-1973 base levels plus a matching amount of old oil, "stripper" oil from extremely low volume wells, and imported crude oil.

EPAA was amended beginning in February 1976 to provide three tiers of prices: lower tier, upper tier, and exempt oil. Lower-tier oil consisted of crude oil extracted from pre-1973 (and in some cases pre-1976) producing properties. Lower-tier oil (and, earlier, old oil) was generally priced in the range of $5–$7 per barrel. Upper-tier oil consisted of crude oil from newer, post-1975, properties and oil produced from older properties in excess of applicable lower-tier base levels. Upper-tier ceiling prices ranged from approximately $11 per barrel to $16 per barrel through the period 1976–early 1981. The highest tier of oil was not subject to price ceilings and consisted of imported crude oil, stripper oil, and certain other minor categories. Exempt oil prices generally followed the path of the unregulated world price of crude oil, which rose from approximately $4 per barrel prior to the embargo to over $35 near the end of controls in early 1981. Under powers granted in 1976, President Carter began a phase-out of crude oil price controls in June 1979, and President Reagan abruptly completed the phase-out in January 1981.

Crude oil price controls were accompanied by ceilings on the prices that refiners, wholesalers, and retailers could charge for refined petroleum products. Refined product price controls were accompanied by allocation regulations governing the flow of supplies. Following the outlines of earlier phases, EPAA allowed certain types of cost increases above a 1973 base to be passed through, dollar for dollar, to the consumer. Except for memorable periods of shortages and gasoline lines, this flexibility quite often allowed ceiling prices to remain above the prices determined in the marketplace by the interplay of supply and demand. Mandatory ceilings on most product prices (except gasoline) were eliminated over 1976–1979.

Regulatory Winners and Losers

Efficiency and Regulation in Oil Markets. Any change in regulatory policy, from initial imposition through decontrol, produces winners and losers because of its effects on the prices, costs, and profits that determine the distribution of income generated in the marketplace.

99

Indeed, this is so well recognized by regulatory decision makers that it implicitly sets the terms of policy debate. The task of every affected interest group is to convince regulators and legislators that social justice demands the group's capture of benefits and protection from economic harm; or that its gains are shared with all at the expense of none, while its losses are the losses of the entire nation. Seldom, however, is the case for or against a given regulation as straightforward as proponents and opponents would portray it.

In addition to affecting the distribution of income, regulatory policies typically change the allocation of resources. Notwithstanding policy makers' objectives of promoting distributional fairness, efficiency in the use of our scarce resources is a desirable goal. Efficiency means allocating the limited resources we have so as to yield the maximum net value to the public as a whole—getting as much benefit as we can at the lowest possible cost. Promoting efficiency and making the aggregate U.S. economic "pie" as large as possible at least raises the possiblity of making everyone better off.

The charges that have been accurately leveled at federal regulation of petroleum prices are that such regulation produced substantial economic inefficiencies in the economy and often did so at the expense of originally targeted beneficiaries. An efficient adaptation to the world ushered in by the Organization of Petroleum Exporting Countries (OPEC) in 1973 required (and continues to require) two primary adjustments in the U.S. economy: (1) a more conservative consumption of energy resources, achieved by forgoing those incremental uses that yield less in benefits than the cost the country bears to acquire its incremental (typically imported) energy supplies; and (2) increased production of those domestic energy resources that can be had at less cost than the incremental supplies they displace. As discussed below, regulations adopted as adjuncts to the basic program of oil price controls were particularly destructive of the first of these objectives; and price controls themselves thwarted achievement of the second. In particular, artificially low prices resulted in both the overconsumption of imported crude oil and the underproduction of domestic petroleum. In addition, domestic price ceilings and associated regulations placed upward pressure on the cost of imported crude oil and created an inordinately expensive administrative, reporting, and enforcement burden.

Price Controls and Oil Production. Unless domestic oil-producing companies are to be viewed as charitable institutions rather than profit-seeking enterprises, they cannot be expected of their own accord to supply crude oil past the point where incremental production adds more to their costs than the price received adds to revenues. Regardless of overall profitability, such production obviously pulls profits down at the margin. Accordingly, by preventing U.S. producers from receiving the price prevailing in the international marketplace, federal price regulations precluded the production of a range of output from domestic oil reserves that could have been had at less cost than the imported oil that replaced it. If the nation could have had an additional barrel of oil at a resource cost (that is, labor, materials, and reduced future availability) of, say, $20, it made little sense to hand over $35 of national wealth to a foreign supplier. Yet, this was precisely the effect of federal price ceilings; and the $15 difference was a pure net loss to the nation's economy without offsetting domestic benefits. The sum of these national losses is estimated to have varied between $1 billion and $5 billion (1982 dollars) per year over 1975–1980. The associated discouragement to domestic oil production and concomitant overconsumption of imported crude oil was in the range of 0.3–1.5 million barrels per day.[3]

The effect of federal price regulations on the level of oil imports was a windfall to foreign sellers of crude oil. Increased U.S. demand and the elimination of the threat of a positive U.S. supply response to monopolistic pricing in the world market played right into the hands of the OPEC cartel. Although numerical estimates of this effect are unavailable, the result was to increase the net cost of controls to the nation. This cost was further increased to the extent that the full cost of imported oil exceeded its price. Although difficult to quantify, divergences between full cost and price could arise, for example, from any national security threats posed by import dependence. For each dollar of such divergences, the estimated annual national losses due to controls over 1975–1980 rises by $100 million–$530 million (1982 dollars).[4] Finally, the full cost imposed by federal regulation of oil prices must include the public and private accounting, record keeping, and legal resources consumed in carrying out the program. Estimates of these costs range from $0.6 billion to $2.0 billion (1982 dollars) per year.[5]

Spreading the Returns to Regulation with Downstream Controls. Notwithstanding uncertainty as to precise figures, it is clear that the inefficiency cost the nation paid for crude oil price controls was substantial. In addition to shrinking the national economic pie, however, federal oil price regulations also redistributed massive amounts of income. The most obvious losers were the stockholders of producing companies and, to some extent, the suppliers of labor, land, and materials used in oil production. If oil producers had been able to sell the output they produced at unregulated prices, they could have realized increased income ranging between $17 billion and $57 billion (1982 dollars) annually over 1975–1980.[6] Although much of this income is still being channeled away from producers and price incentives are being held below market levels by the Windfall Profits (that is, excise) Tax, decontrol in 1981 did raise price incentives and, accordingly, oil development efforts rose sharply.

With tens of billions of dollars per year effectively under the control of federal regulators, competition in the political arena for accesss to those funds was understandably intense and, unfortunately, wasteful. The major competitors were the users of crude oil. The return they sought was the ability to consume or resell price-controlled crude oil valued at unregulated market prices. The competitors for regulatory returns ranged from the large, integrated oil refiners and smaller, independent refiners to wholesalers, retailers, and final consumers. As ultimately formulated, the regulatory scheme for allocating price-controlled oil gave each of these competing groups portions, albeit notably unequal, of the income transferred away from domestic crude oil producers by price controls.

As initially devised, federal regulations allowed access to price-controlled crude oil to be determined primarily on the basis of existing and historical contracts that linked crude oil producers and refiners. This was to the great benefit of those fortunate refiners who found themselves tied, through either explicit contracts or vertical integration, to suppliers of price-controlled crude oil. The billions of dollars denied to crude oil producers by price regulation were directly transferred into profits for certain domestic refiners to the extent that low-cost price-controlled crude oil could be resold, upon refining, at prices set by market forces. Very little of the private benefits of access to price-controlled crude oil reached the general consuming public.

As noted, controls on oil prices were originally intended to serve the public by holding down inflation. With the passage of EPAA, the purpose became more explicitly to soften the blow of the Arab oil embargo and the associated jump in oil prices on oil consumers. By themselves, however, crude oil price controls did nothing to restrain intermediate or final consumer prices. Unless strictly regulated, the marketplace dictates that these prices be based on the cost to refiners of their incremental crude oil supplies. Notwithstanding differences among refiners in their access to price-controlled crude oil and, hence, their *average* crude oil costs, all refiners' incremental supplies of crude oil came from the unregulated sector of the market. The supplies of price-controlled crude oil were never sufficient to yield the amount of products that refiners wanted to sell. Moreover, profit-seeking refiners were induced to refine more than their acquired supplies of price-controlled oil only so long as the prices received for products derived

102

from additional crude oil added at least as much to revenues as the cost of buying and processing that uncontrolled crude oil. Like crude oil producers, oil refiners are not primarily charitable institutions. They bought and refined price-exempt crude oil because the prices they received on resulting products were sufficient to cover the costs. Consequently, with unregulated refined product prices based on the prices of exempt crude oil and with all units of a product priced the same in an unregulated market, fortunate refiners with access to price-controlled oil were not forced by crude oil price controls to pass along any of the difference between market and ceiling crude oil prices to downstream buyers.

In short, crude oil controls did nothing to hold down consumers' oil prices and general inflation. Any success on these objectives would have had to come from effective ceilings on refined product prices. As actually promulgated, EPAA price controls were ostensibly designed to force refiners to base their prices on their *average*, rather than incremental, costs. The provisions of these controls that enabled refiners to pass through costs, however, were generally lenient enough to allow legal maximum prices to exceed the prices determined by the marketplace. In certain circumstances, price ceilings were more binding than the marketplace for refiners but not for downstream marketers. In such cases, those marketers fortunate enough to be tied to price-constrained refiners were able to capture significant portions of the income transferred away from crude oil producers by price controls—in a manner exactly paralleling that of unconstrained refiners with access to controlled crude oil.[7]

The flexibility of refined product price ceilings was fortunate for the economy as a whole, although not necessarily for particular buyers of petroleum products. When refined product price ceilings were more binding than the marketplace, prices ceased to serve their crucial function of balancing supply and demand. Artificially low prices discouraged supply and encouraged demand. The necessary results were shortages, with automobile drivers wasting hours in gasoline lines, truckers and oil marketers marching on Washington, and farmers lacking fuel to work their fields. Although collected price statistics may have shown lower prices, binding ceilings left the real prices of oil products to consumers—pump prices *plus* the value of wasted time and lost crops—higher than they otherwise would have been.

Power, Priorities, and Allocation Controls

Shortages in some domestic refined petroleum markets were reported as early as April 1972—considerably prior to the disruptions to supply brought on by the Arab oil embargo of late 1973.[8] Moreover, unequal access to price-controlled crude oil and haphazardly binding downstream controls produced gross inequalities in the shares of politically redistributed income captured by intermediate and final oil consumers. In addition, price-constrained sellers of oil found themselves having to ration their supplies. For sound business reasons, such sellers preferred to retain long-standing customers, which led to charges of discrimination. The embargo and sharp rise in unregulated oil prices in late 1973 only served to exaggerate these sorts of distortions and anomalies. Perceived distortions and anomalies provided useful ammunition to interest groups with poor direct or indirect access to price-controlled crude oil. These groups responded by putting well-aimed pressure on federal policy makers to have crude oil and refined product supplies allocated more "equitably" by an explicit regulatory mechanism.[9]

If not by design, then at least in practice, interested parties' notions of "equitable" most typically meant priority access to price-controlled crude oil. Any petroleum user able to "go to the head of the line," so to speak, realized real benefits from access to oil at less than unregulated market prices. The ultimate outcome of the political pressure to establish access by priority rankings was, under EPAA, a far-reaching and complex system of supply allocation. For refined products, this system included the assigning of suppliers to buyers, formulas for determining supply sharing, priority designations for selected groups, and an extremely large regulatory bureaucracy with formal and informal discretion to direct the flow of petroleum among intermediate and final users.

The clear beneficiaries from the federal regulation of petroleum product allocations were those interest groups able to establish themselves, through political means, as high-priority purchasers. Foremost among these were independent petroleum wholesale and retail marketers, the agricultural sector, and utility and industrial suppliers and purchasers of fuel oil.[10]

Several observations are revealing on the source and nature of the benefits derived from regulations by these groups. First, typical gasoline consumers form a broad and diffuse group that is poorly represented in the roll of campaign contributors and lobby organizations. Accordingly, they were given very low priority under EPAA allocation and left to suffer through gas lines in 1973–1974 and 1979, all the while being told by government officials and oil companies alike that the shortages they were bearing were the fault of their own improvident driving habits and the greed of foreign oil sellers, rather than federal regulations that prevented prices from balancing supply and demand. Second, concentrated and well-organized interest groups were able to use allocation controls to direct increased supplies to their sectors and thereby drive down prices even when supplies were otherwise available at unregulated market-clearing prices. This was the result, for example, when the Department of Energy's Special Rule Number 9 forced reallocations of diesel fuel to farm regions in spring 1979.[11] Third, petroleum product marketers and agricultural representatives were back within months after decontrol in 1981 lobbying Congress for a new allocation system. Interest groups heavily dependent on automobile travel (for example, hotel operators) had apparently learned from EPAA experience and lobbied against such a system.[12]

The essence of the stakes involved in the federal allocation of petroleum supplies was exhibited with unusual candor in the following exchange between a U.S. senator and a representative of food distributors during recent hearings on the possible reimposition of price and allocation controls:[13]

> *Senator:* Do you think you would be better off if we had no allocation and allowed you to compete with the rest of the marketplace?
> *Food Distributor:* I think that is true . . . but for a severe, long-run problem I believe there needs to be an allocation program.
> *Senator:* An allocation program if it gets your priority in. If you couldn't you probably wouldn't be in favor of it?
> *Food Distributor:* We would be in favor of no allocation program.
>
> . . . .
>
> *Senator:* Are Senators on that [priority] list?
> *Food Distributor:* You will have to take care of yourself, Senator.

The allocation system adopted in the 1970s in order to deal with distortions created by price regulation may or may not have been equitable, depending on the standards of fairness we wish to apply. There is no question, however, about the economic consequences of the system for the nation's economy as a whole: allocation regulations thwarted the efficient use and distribution of petroleum products and thereby generated significant net economic losses. There were at least four significant sources of such losses.

First, allocation regulations were a block to competition.[14] The assigning of suppliers to buyers and the creation of base-level supply obligations left suppliers less able and/or less willing to take on new customers and inhibited the "shopping around" by buyers that is such a potent enforcer of competition. Second, allocation regulations encouraged overconsumption of petroleum products and insufficient use of alternative fuels by high-priority users able to satisfy their demand at less than market prices. Low-priority users, on the other hand, underconsumed petroleum and were encouraged to invest excessively in protection against shortages. Third, the extremely complicated regulation of oil allocations contributed significantly to the paperwork and bureaucratic costs of the federal price control program that were noted previously. Last, allocation regulations and the associated authority of regulators to change those regulations were particularly distortive of cost-saving business practices. Although quantitative measures are difficult to come by, it is clear from the hiring, promotion, and personnel-assigning strategies of oil-using companies that regulation altered the practices that were conducive to their survival and profit opportunities. As a result of the regulatory process, the fate of a firm depended relatively more than it otherwise would have on its ability to "produce" favorable rulings and regulations, as opposed to its ability to produce refined products, oil marketing services, or the goods and services made from petroleum products. Resources so devoted to the competition that merely sliced up the spoils of regulation reduced the level of goods and services that could be produced by the nation's economy.

Subsidies and Special Interests under the Entitlements Program

Equalizing Effects on Refiners. Federal allocation regulations expanded the list of those who might benefit from the regulation of oil prices. By themselves, however, these regulations could not eliminate large disparities in refiners' average crude oil costs. Refiners with good and frozen-by-regulation historical access to price-controlled domestic crude oil had lower average costs than, for example, refiners whose only source of supply was price-exempt imported crude oil. When refined product price ceilings were binding, inequalities were manifested in the anomalies of refiner-specific shortages and of different prices charged by different sellers for the same product sold in the same market at the same time.[15] When product price ceilings were not more binding than the marketplace, refiners' cost inequalities showed up as sharp differences in their profitability.

To counteract differences in refiners' input prices and the profits derived from crude oil price controls, federal regulators created a so-called Entitlements Program in November 1974.[16] As much as any other aspect of federal regulation of the petroleum sector, this program was the harbor of the special interests that made it so hard to eliminate petroleum price regulations.

The Entitlements Program had as its central objective the equalization of crude oil costs to domestic refiners. It accomplished this through a process that allocated rights to refine price-controlled crude oil on an approximately equiproportionate basis to all refiners, without requiring the actual transshipment of oil. A refiner with relatively good access to controlled oil (and, thus, lower than the national-average crude oil cost) was required to purchase "entitlements" to any amount of price-controlled crude oil that it processed in excess of the amount that the refiner would have processed had it used controlled and exempt crude oils in their national average proportions. Entitlements were purchased from those refiners with relatively poor access to price-controlled crude oil (and, thus, higher than the national-average crude oil cost). In this way, the average input costs of both low-cost and high-cost refiners were moved toward the national average. The price and number of entitlements were set by regulation to ensure that this movement left all refiners with roughly the same cost—the national average.

The Entitlements Program was a boon to those refiners otherwise having poor links to the sellers of low-cost price-controlled crude oil. Not surprisingly, over its life and even after its death in January 1981, the Entitlements Program was repeatedly challenged in the courts and regulatory proceedings by refiners who, whether by luck or foresight, had especially good access to price-controlled crude oil. In its essentials, the program allowed the federal regulatory apparatus to capture from this group of refiners the $17 billion to $57 billion generated each year by crude oil price controls. These sums were then redistributed to all refiners on a roughly equal basis. This redistribution by itself need not have had significant effects on the economy's use of petroleum resources. The manner in which it was accomplished, however, did have important economic consequences.

Promoting Oil Consumption and Import Dependence. The most striking effect of the Entitlements Program was a heavy subsidy to all U.S. refiners for the importation of foreign crude oil.[17] This subsidy arose because the program ensured all refiners buying crude oil at completely unregulated prices that such oil would end up costing no more per barrel than the entitlements-equalized cost of all crude oil refined in the country. Incremental purchases of price-exempt imported crude oil lowered the proportion of price-controlled oil used by a refiner. Thus, the *net* incremental cost of imported oil was its price *minus* the attendant increase in entitlements sales (for a high-cost, entitlements-selling refiner) or the attendant savings on required entitlements purchases (for a low-cost, entitlements-buying refiner). Despite stated national goals of "energy independence," this effective subsidy consistently ranged between 10 percent and 20 percent of the price of each barrel of imported crude oil over 1975–1980.

It is tempting to infer that the entitlements subsidy to crude oil imports was an unintended result. The Entitlements Program, however, was originally proposed and lobbied for by the *buyers* of refiners' products.[18] Downstream buyers stood to benefit because the effect of the Entitlements Program's subsidy on the incremental cost of crude oil to refiners provided incentives for them to increase their output of refined petroleum products. In fact, the increased supply on the market of most of these products acted to reduce prices below what they otherwise would have been and thereby encouraged consumption.[19] This directly contradicted the objective of improving energy conservation and imposed substantial losses on the nation's economy.

Efficiency in the use of crude oil requires that the full cost borne by the nation to acquire a barrel of crude oil not exceed the value that buyers place on the contribution of that oil to the incremental refined products they consume. Independent of any subsidies to domestic refiners, the full cost to the nation of the crude oil needed to satisfy subsidized consumption was its unregulated world market price plus any additional (for example, national security) costs of import dependence. Petroleum users seeing artificially low, subsidized, prices as their private costs were induced to buy oil for all uses that yielded personal benefits at least as great as these costs. Thus, there was a range of oil consumption that yielded less in total benefits to the nation's citizens than the costs they incurred. With an entitlements-subsidized private cost of crude oil of approximately $30 per barrel in 1980, for example, the country as a whole was giving up $35 of national wealth to foreign suppliers in exchange for only $30 worth of incremental benefits. The $5 difference was a net loss to the country. The total of these losses is estimated to have varied between $0.3 billion and $1.2 billion (1982 dollars) per year over 1975–1980. The associated increase in crude oil imports used to satisfy subsidized demand was in the range of 0.8 million–1.3 million barrels per day.[20]

The noted increase in oil imports under the Entitlements Program was in addition to the increase caused by the depressing effect of price controls on domestic crude oil production. The results were further support for the OPEC cartel and upward pressure on international prices. This effect did not go unnoticed in the world. Indeed, a central reason for President Carter's eventual acquiescence in 1979 to a plan of phased price deregulation was strong pressure from oil-consuming allies who found themselves forced to pay high international crude oil prices that were, to some unmeasurable degree, the responsibility of U.S. domestic regulatory policy. Any entitlements-induced increases in imported oil prices were a source of U.S. losses to be added to those arising from the noted subsidy-induced overconsumption of oil. The net national cost of the Entitlements Program was further increased to the extent that the full cost to the country of imported oil exceeded its price. Every one dollar of a premium due to, say, national security costs attendant on imported oil would have generated annual national losses of $300 million–$500 million (1982 dollars) over 1975–1980.[21] Finally, the Entitlements Program was a major contributor to the overall costs of administering and enforcing the system of petroleum price regulation. In short, the program did not perform well against standards of national economic well-being.

The Targeting of Special Interests. The artificially low prices for petroleum products that were produced by the Entitlements Program were a benefit to both intermediate and final oil consumers. Specific effects depended on the extent to which market forces of supply and demand resulted in the successive pass-through of subsidized incremental costs along the stream leading to end users. Domestic refiners, themselves, appear to have captured roughly 60 percent of the billions under the control of the Entitlements Program.[22] The remainder went to wholesalers, retailers, and, to some degree, final consumers.

Interestingly, the substantial gains of refiners gave lie to the image of a monolithic lobby of "big oil." Even among the largest integrated companies, the effect of federal policy was disparate. As the balance of operations shifted from domestic crude oil production (where regulatory burdens were imposed) to refining and international operations (where entitlements benefits were conferred), companies acquired vested interests in the overall regulatory program—as differences in companies' lobbying efforts on the issue of decontrol repeatedly testified. With respect to downstream beneficiaries of the entitlements subsidy, the history of rule making and legislative hearings suggests the identity of the interest groups that were best able to recognize and act upon the gains at stake. These included fuel oil marketers, electric utilities, the airline industry, organized labor, the agricultural sector, and certain petrochemical manufacturers.

In addition to its general subsidy to crude oil refining, the Entitlements Program was laced with special subsidiary programs directly targeted to specific interests. Among these were explicit and implicit subsidies to refiners able to demonstrate financial hardship, refiners of low-quality California crude oil, producers of exotic substitutes for petroleum (for example, trash burned for electricity generation), and the federal government's own strategic oil stockpile program. Most notable among the special programs were (1) subsidies to the importation of heavy fuel oil into the East Coast and, at times, to imports of middle distillate products (for example, home heating oil); and (2) extra grants of valuable, salable entitlements to small refiners.

Entitlements subsidies to imported refined petroleum products lowered the incremental costs of such products. The direct beneficiaries were wholesale marketers. These marketers, in fact, proposed such subsidies and effectively achieved their adoption. Retail marketers and final customers also benefited, as lower incremental wholesale costs were translated into lower market prices. The consequences, however, were reduced conservation efforts and distortions to the mix of fuels consumed. In particular, subsidized heavy fuel oil prices contributed to the electric power industry's marked sluggishness in converting to coal, despite otherwise sound economics and federal mandates.

The history of U.S. oil policy indicates that one of the most consistently successful special-interest lobbies has been the group of smaller, independent, domestic refiners. This group, for example, was singled out for highly lucrative and preferential treatment under the system of oil import controls in place from 1959 through early 1973. In addition, certain components of the allocation part of the federal oil price control scheme, such as the buy/sell program requiring major refiners to supply others with crude oil, were designed explicitly for the benefit of small refiners. In terms of dollars captured and economic impact, however, the Small Refiner Bias in the Entitlements Program was the most important form of regulatory support yet attained by this group.

The Small Refiner Bias amounted to a system of cash payments to small refiners, made out of the funds transferred away from crude oil producers by price controls and earned solely by virtue of being small. Small refiners were those with a smaller capacity than 175,000 barrels per day, and the bias encompassed all but 22 of the approximately 150 domestic refiners. Eligible refiners were given extra grants of salable entitlements according to a sliding scale that provided proportionately more entitlements as size decreased. As table 6–1 indicates, when the value of an entitlement peaked in mid-1980, eligible refiners were realizing subsidies of up to $31 million per year. After accounting for the typically higher costs of small refiners, net gains for a refiner with a capacity of 30,000 barrels per day were running in the range of $20 million–$25 million per year.

The Small Refiner Bias was officially justified as a means of preserving a group of firms able to enforce competition in the domestic refining industry. This justification is less than compelling. Small re-

TABLE 6–1

SUBSIDIES UNDER
THE SMALL REFINER BIAS, MAY 1980

Refiner Size (millions of barrels/day)			Annual Value of Bias (millions of dollars)		
0	to	10	$0	to	$22.9
10+	to	30	$22.9	to	$31.2
30+	to	50	$31.2	to	$20.9
50+	to	100	$20.9	to	$12.6
100+	to	175	$12.6	to	$0

SOURCE: Based on data in U.S. Department of Energy, *Monthly Energy Review*, September 1980.

fineries, particularly those that could survive only with hefty subsidies, generally operate at higher costs than their larger counterparts. Thus, competition could be promoted only at the price to the nation of refined petroleum produced at higher than minimum achievable cost. Moreover, the most effective enforcers of competition in U.S. petroleum product markets appear to be the numerous domestic refiners who can survive without subsidies and the brokers and wholesalers who are able to tap into the large set of refiners operating in the international marketplace.

The effectiveness of the small refiner lobby has been founded to a significant extent on its ability to portray itself as a poor David facing the Goliath of "big oil." And, indeed, the termination of the Small Refiner Bias upon decontrol in January 1981 has led to the demise of a number of small firms that had prospered under regulation. The image, however, of the "rich and powerful" gaining at the expense of the "poor and weak" in the deregulated market is misleading. A significant number of small refiners are, in fact, subsidiaries of Fortune 500 companies. Even more typically, small refiners are private or closely held public firms, whose owners include some of the wealthiest families in the United States. Ownership of large refineries, on the other hand, is fairly widely dispersed across income classes as a result of substantial stockholding by pension funds, life insurance companies, and other institutional investors.

The Small Refiner Bias in the Entitlements Program gave the owners of small refineries larger pieces of the national economic pie. At the same time, however, the inefficiencies it created reduced the total size of that pie. Small refineries, by their design, do not take full advantage of available economies of scale. Moreover, their output typically tilts

111

toward relatively low-valued heavy products, and they are relatively poor at reducing the sulfur and lead contents of fuels. Thus, the artificial subsidization of small refiners distorted the petroleum product mix desired by the economy and thwarted achievement of environmental goals. Any given level and mix of petroleum product output and any given set of environmental goals could have been realized more cheaply if federal regulation had not propped up inefficient refiners. The difference between the cost the country incurred to supply itself with petroleum products and the minimum cost it could have incurred was a waste of national resources.

The Small Refiner Bias, refined product import entitlements, special subsidiary programs for other selected interest groups, and the Entitlement Program's substantial subsidy to the refining of imported oil were all the products of the political competition for the financial benefits of access to price-controlled domestic crude oil. It was inevitable that the resulting distribution of benefits would create vested interests in the federal program of oil price regulation. It would have been quixotic to expect entitlements beneficiaries to recognize the negative effects of this program on the nation's economy and to respond by supporting deregulation.

Conclusion: The Politics and Economics
of Regulatory Reform

The central thread running through the recent history of U.S. oil price policy is the use of federal regulation to block substantial portions of the transfer of income, which would otherwise occur in the marketplace, from the intermediate and final users of crude oil to the producers of crude oil. Reasonable people can easily disagree on whether this objective is justified on the grounds of fairness. It is far more difficult, however, to disagree with the conclusion that the methods actually employed in pursuit of this goal have had significantly adverse effects on the health of the national economy. Under the system of regulation in place from 1971 to 1981, these effects were the result of regulation-induced inefficiencies in the allocation of energy resources. Price controls, allocation regulations, and the Entitlements Program led the economy to overconsume imported crude oil, underproduce domestic crude oil, distort the distribution and mix of refined products, prop up inefficient refiners and the OPEC cartel, pervert the nature of competition and business dealings in the petroleum sector, and expend excessive resources on regulatory administration and implementation. The attendant annual waste of national resources was in the billions of dollars.

The complexity, pervasiveness, and longevity of the program of federal regulation of petroleum prices, despite the evident economic effects, contain useful lessons for the design of regulatory reform. Most obviously, the general interest the public has in the performance of the overall economy is not identical to the private interests of individuals. While regulation may have been designed to benefit the broad sector of the public who are the users of crude oil, these "users" are a markedly heterogeneous group. Divergences in their private interests ended up being mediated by the federal regulatory apparatus, with each round of competition typically producing not only more regulation with more distortions but also new vested interests. As a result, the decision to decontrol produced long and rancorous political battles. The eventual arrival of decontrol reflected the mounting evidence of economic waste from regulation; an economy not performing well in response to the energy problem; the ability of congressional policy makers to introduce a politically difficult decision in phases over a period longer than their terms of office and to leave the final decision to the president; pressure from international allies; and the fortuitous timing of legislated authority for presidential action early in a president's term.[23]

Finally, the interest groups with stakes in price regulation have not disappeared. They recently secured the passage of legislation providing for the emergency reimposition of EPAA-style price and allocation regulations—though the act was vetoed by President Reagan. Meanwhile, federal policy continues to capture billions of dollars of income that would otherwise accrue to domestic crude oil producers, now using direct taxes rather than price controls and leaving the Congress and the Treasury, rather than the Department of Energy, to allocate the proceeds. Thus the arenas may be changing, but the battles between interest groups over oil policy will most likely continue.

Notes

1. These policies are described and analyzed in detail in Joseph P. Kalt, *The Economics and Politics of Oil Price Regulation* (Cambridge, Mass.: MIT Press, 1981).

2. Examples of this conclusion, particularly with respect to price regulation, are found in Kenneth J. Arrow and Joseph P. Kalt, *Petroleum Price Regulation: Should We Decontrol?* (Washington, D.C.: American Enterprise Institute, 1979); Ford Foundation, *Energy: The Next Twenty Years* (Cambridge, Mass.: Ballinger, 1979), pp. 185-99; and Robert Stobaugh and Daniel Yergin, eds., *Energy Future* (New York: Random House, 1979), pp. 41-55.

3. These estimates are developed in Kalt, *The Economics and Politics of Oil Price Regulation*, pp. 187-208.

4. These estimates are based on the estimated increments to U.S. demand for imported oil noted above, discussed in ibid., pp. 192-94 and 205-8; possible divergences

between the private cost and the full cost of imported oil are examined on pp. 221-32 and in Stobaugh and Yergin, *Energy Future*, pp. 16-55.

5. These figures are based on data provided by Paul W. MacAvoy, ed., *Federal Energy Administration Regulation: Report of the Presidential Task Force* (Washington, D.C.: American Enterprise Institute, 1977), and are developed in Kalt, *The Economics and Politics of Oil Price Regulation*, pp. 208-13.

6. Based on results reported in Kalt, *The Economics and Politics of Oil Price Regulation*, pp. 213-21.

7. The interaction of crude and refined petroleum price regulations is examined by E. Allen Jacobs, "Essays on the Regulation of U.S. Petroleum Markets, 1971-1981" (Ph.D. diss., Massachusetts Institute of Technology, 1981), and by Scott Harvey and Calvin T. Roush, Jr., *Petroleum Product Price Regulations: Output, Efficiency, and Competitive Effects* (Federal Trade Commission, 1981).

8. Reports of shortages appear in Platt's *Oilgram Price Service*, April 26, 1972, p. 3.

9. Charles R. Owens, "The History of Petroleum Price Controls in Office of Economic Stabilization, U.S. Treasury Department," *Historical Working Papers: 8/15/71 to 4/30/74* (U.S. Treasury Department, 1974).

10. The most detailed analysis to date of the political activities of these groups is found in Carol A. Forti, "The Money, Power, and Politics of Oil Supply Disruptions" (Brookings Institution, Washington, D.C., 1982, manuscript).

11. The 1979 episode is examined by Stephen E. Erfle, John Pound, and Joseph P. Kalt, "The Use of Political Pressure as a Policy Tool During the 1979 Oil Supply Crisis" Discussion Paper E-80-09 (Cambridge, Mass.: Kennedy School of Government, Harvard University, 1980). Further insights are offered by Philip K. Verleger, Jr., "A Review of the U.S. Petroleum Crisis of 1979" (Brookings Institution, Washington, D.C., 1979, manuscript).

12. See, for example, testimony by the representative of Holiday Inns, Inc., in U.S. Senate, Committee on Energy and National Resources, *Government Responses to Oil Supply Disruptions, Hearings*, 1981, pp. 561-67.

13. This exchange is taken from U.S. Senate, Committee on Energy and Natural Resources, *Government Responses to Oil Supply Disruptions*, p. 602.

14. The anticompetitive effects of these regulations are analyzed in MacAvoy, *Federal Energy Administration Regulation*, and Harvey and Roush, *Petroleum Product Price Regulations*.

15. Anomalies of this type are noted in Douglas Bohi and Milton Russell, *Limiting Oil Imports: An Economic History and Analysis* (Baltimore: Johns Hopkins University Press, 1978), pp. 208-30.

16. See the *U.S. Code of Federal Regulations*, Title 10, 211.67.

17. This subsidy is noted in Rand Corporation, *Petroleum Regulation: The False Dilemma of Decontrol* (Santa Monica, Calif.: Rand Corporation, 1977). This study argues that the Entitlements Program's subsidy to crude oil refining had no effect on consumer prices of petroleum. Evidence reported in Kalt, *The Economics and Politics of Oil Price Regulation*, pp. 103-85, indicates that a substantial portion of the Entitlements Program's subsidy was passed through to consumer prices.

18. See Craufurd D. Goodwin, ed., *Energy Policy in Perspective: Today's Problems, Yesterday's Solutions* (Washington, D.C.: Brookings Institution, 1981), p. 470.

19. This conclusion is based on evidence reported in Kalt, *The Economics and Politics of Oil Price Regulation*, pp. 103-85.

20. These estimates are developed in ibid., pp. 188-94.

21. These estimates are based on the estimated increments to U.S. demand for imported oil noted above, see note 20.

22. See note 17 above.

23. The decontrol decision is reported in Goodwin, *Energy Policy in Perspective*, pp. 475-636.

7

The Political Economy
of Federal Regulation
# of Surface Transportation

MARCUS ALEXIS

Economic regulation of surface transportation at the federal level dates from 1887 with the enactment of the Interstate Commerce Act, which, among other things, established the Interstate Commerce Commission (ICC). The ICC is thus the oldest of the federal regulatory agencies and the model for many of the subsequent state and federal economic regulatory bodies. The history of the ICC is a textbook case of the use of governmental regulation to resolve the conflicting claims of economic interest groups, and to achieve through the exercise of the political process advantages that could not be attained through market competition. The results have been transfers of wealth to successful interest groups, the creation of excess capacity, higher than competitive prices, delays in introducing new technologies, and management practices that emphasize the manipulation of the regulatory process rather than efficient management of scarce and valuable resources. What interest groups have gained has come at great cost to the public.

Federal Regulation of Railroads

The Interstate Commerce Act was enacted in response to agitation by shippers and railroad executives for federal intervention in the interstate railroad industry. Rail executives were concerned about rate wars, secret concessions, and rebates. Attempts to stabilize the industry by a series of cartel-like pooling arrangements before 1880 proved to be of limited success. Shippers were unhappy with practices that resulted in rate instability (not necessarily higher rates, because rates were, on the average, declining). Shippers also objected because short hauls were in many instances more costly than long hauls. Both sides advocated legislation that would require publication of rates and advance notice (a waiting period) before rate increases or decreases would become effective.[1] Though agreed on the "need" for federal intervention, shippers and railroad representatives had quite different approaches to the proposed intervention; each group sought to weight the balance in its own favor.

Beginning with Illinois in 1871, several states passed legislation regulating railroads and other public interest businesses. Railroad regulatory agencies were empowered to set maximum charges, prevent discrimination and extortion, and prevent the merger of parallel lines.[2] These laws were upheld by a series of U.S. Supreme Court decisions in 1877.[3]

Railroad executives, shippers, politicians, and economists (notably the economist Charles Francis Adams, Jr., and Arthur T. Hadley, president of the American Economic Association, 1898–1899) pushed for a unified system of federal regulation to replace the often conflicting and inconsistent state laws. On the whole, the railroad representatives were in favor of legislation that would disallow secret price concessions and rebates. But they wished unambiguously to legalize the pooling of revenue, equipment, and freight. The politicians were divided on the merits of such regulation and deferred to the "expert" advice of the railroad people and economists, who for the most part (particularly Adams and Hadley) thought that competition was unworkable in the railroad industry because of its large investment requirements, the high ratio of fixed to variable costs, and the limited number of lines connecting points.[4]

By 1880, federal legislation to regulate the railroads had won popular support; the debate was on the form this legislation would take. There was active lobbying on both sides—railroads and shippers. Their interests were opposed on many basic issues, but carriers and shippers both sought an end to the rate instability of the 1880s.[5] What the regulation would include would be determined in the political arena.

In 1877, Congressman Reagan of Texas introduced the bill which was to become the Interstate Commerce Act of 1887. It took seven years for the bill to pass the House of Representatives and another three before it was reconciled with a measure introduced in the Senate.[6] The Reagan bill differed from the Senate bill in several significant ways.

1. The House preferred administration of the act by the courts, whereas the Senate envisioned establishment of the Interstate Commerce Commission.

2. The House wanted a prohibition against pooling; the Senate preferred that it not be outlawed.

3. The Senate favored a weak and elastic long- and short-haul clause, and the House an absolute prohibition againt charging more for a short haul than for a long.

4. The House preferred a more specific prohibition against rebating than the Senate.[7]

In 1887, members of the Senate were elected by the respective state legislatures, whereas House members were elected directly. Thus, senators were less vulnerable to popular opinion. Effective industry work at the legislative level, where benefits could be concentrated on a limited number of legislators (and the costs imposed on a separate and diffuse consumer group), provided favorable conditions for legislative "capture" by the interest groups.[8]

The architects of the Reagan bill were E. J. Patterson, a Pennsylvania oil man, and George B. Hibbard, attorney for the Petroleum Producers' Union, a group of shippers in the Pennsylvania oil fields. The proposed legislation reflected intraindustry rivalry. It was directed at both the railroads and the Standard Oil Trust; the latter enjoyed advantages not available to smaller shippers.[9] The Senate bill was supported by the railroads and the economist Charles Francis Adams, Jr., who framed it.

The railroad interests won on all the major issues save one, pooling. The final bill established a commission that had a high degree of discretion, authorized the commission to grant exemption from the long- and short-haul "prohibition," and prohibited pooling arrangements.

The ICC Act as finally passed contained eight major sections:

Sec. 1: All rates were to be "reasonable and just." Unjust and unreasonable charges were prohibited and declared unlawful.

Sec. 2: Preferential treatment of individuals by special rates, rebates, drawbacks, or other devices was declared "unjust discrimination" and made unlawful.

Sec. 3: Undue or unreasonable preference or advantage to any person, company, firm, area, or type of traffic was prohibited.

Sec. 4: It was made illegal to charge more for a short haul than for a longer one, but the ICC could grant an exemption when a railroad was faced with competition.

Sec. 5: Pooling of traffic or earnings was prohibited.

Sec. 6: Railroads were required to print and keep for public inspection schedules of rates and charges for passengers and freight, and classifications of freight. Rate increases required ten days notice. Decreases were subject to immediate publication, but could be made without notice. It was made illegal to charge more or less than the published rate. All tariffs were to be filed with the ICC.

SEC. 7: Railroads were prohibited from breaking continuous movements of freight in an effort to circumvent the act.

SEC. 8: Carriers were to be liable for damages for violation of the act.

The perils of legislative solutions to market realities soon became evident to the drafters of the act. Senate supporters wanted to permit long- and short-haul disparities when railroads were faced with competition from the waterways. But the Supreme Court read the compromise language differently and ruled in 1897 that the exemption was applicable only when railroads were in direct competition with each other. Because the practice of charging lower rates for longer hauls reflected the absence of competition on short hauls, and its presence on longer ones, this interpretation of the statute was exactly the opposite of what the railroads wanted.

The 1887 act did not empower the ICC to set maximum rate levels, nor did it impose a public utility regulatory structure on the railroad industry. Rates of return were not regulated, although rates were to be "reasonable and just." But the 1887 act was the first step in the legislative cartelization of the railroad industry. This first step was followed by a series of amendments strengthening ICC control over the industry and making it in effect the referee of cartel disputes, a role which lasted for eighty-nine years, until the passage of the Railroad Revitalization and Regulatory Reform Act (4R Act) of 1976 and its successor, the Staggers Rail Act of 1980.

The Elkins Act (1903) amended the ICC Act to make railroads prosecutable for rate discrimination, to make beneficiaries of favors liable for penalties, and to make deviation from published rates unlawful. The Hepburn Act (1906) gave the ICC maximum rate jurisdiction, established a thirty-day notice period for rate changes and made rebate recipients liable for treble damages. The Mann-Elkins Act (1910) strengthened, and from the railroad's perspective corrected, ICC discretion in long- and short-haul disputes and gave the ICC power for the first time to suspend (disallow) proposed rates. In the Transportation Act of 1920, Congress empowered the ICC to regulate minimum rates, entry, exit, capital formation, changes of control, and mergers. What had been a private cartel now became a publicly controlled one. The job was completed with the passage of the Reed Bulwinkle Act of 1948, which empowered the ICC to exempt from prosecution under the Sherman Act collective rate making (price fixing) by railroads under its jurisdiction.

The chronicle of events that led to the regulation of railroads can be explained by interest groups seeking to use public power for private gains—wealth transfers. The notion that groups seek to use the political process to secure economic benefits is central to the "capture" theory of regulation formulated by Stigler and Peltzman as well as the "rent-seeking" approach of Krueger;[10] it gains empirical support from the creation and continuation of ICC regulation.

Federal Regulation of Trucking: The Motor Carrier Act of 1935

Not surprisingly, the first advocates of federal regulation of interstate trucking were their economic rivals, the railroads. After World War I the trucking industry grew rapidly. It became a potent rival of the ICC-administered railroad cartel and threatened to disrupt it. The railroads argued that if entry could be limited and rates regulated, "order" could be restored—that is, the cartel could be stabilized. By 1935 many spokesmen for the trucking industry also supported a statutory system of government controls. Supporters of regulation that would put limitations on entry included what is now the American Trucking Association (ATA). A hodgepodge of state regulations, excess capacity exacerbated by the depression, and the realization that federal regulation might benefit those already in the industry by limiting new entry were among the factors that led to this change from earlier trucking industry opposition to federal regulation.

Between 1925 and 1935, Congress showed an increasing interest in extending coverage of the Interstate Commerce Act to the motor carrier segment of the transportation industry. During this decade, Congress considered more than twenty-five bills to extend regulatory coverage in this area but failed to pass any of them. The Interstate Commerce Commission was also investigating the motor carrier industry anew. In 1930 it launched a major study of the industry, its second.

The commission's second study concluded in 1932 with the issuance of a lengthy report, *Coordination of Motor Transportation.*[11] The commission recommended that interstate motor transportation be made subject to full economic regulation at the federal level. A year later, to address the crisis facing the transportation industry, Congress passed the Emergency Railroad Transportation Act of 1933,[12] which created the office of Federal Coordinator of Transportation, whose duty was to make a study of means for "improving conditions surrounding transportation in all its forms and the preparation of plans therefore."[13] The ICC commissioner, Joseph B. Eastman, was named coordinator, and his report, a large part of which was devoted to the proposal to regulate interstate motor carriers, was submitted to the Senate on March 10, 1934.[14] The draft bill included in the coordinator's report formed the basis of the Motor Carrier Act of 1935, which contained the basic rate and entry control provisions later enacted.

The rationale for inclusion of a motor carrier licensing requirement in the federal regulatory scheme was the observation that virtually all other attempts to regulate motor transportation by the states and by foreign nations included such provisions.[15] The implication was that state control of entry had worked well and was necessary for a successful overall system of regulation. In his report, Commissioner Eastman noted that intrastate regulation had generally been successful and had resulted in stabilization of operations and improvement in facilities and service.[16] This report affirmed many of the conclusions regarding "destructive competition" between the regulated and unregulated transportation industry segments earlier reached in the commission's 1932 report.

In the Motor Carrier Act of 1935, Congress identified as one of its primary goals the introduction of a greater degree of order and stability in the motor carrier industry. As was true with respect to railroads forty-eight years earlier, when the Interstate Commerce Act was passed, stability was viewed as important to both shippers and carriers. Regulation was imposed in three areas: (1) entry, (2) rates, and (3) securities, acquisitions, and related financial transactions and agreements. Congress sought to stabilize motor carrier operations by reducing the number of small operators with weak attachments to the industry; it accomplished this by limiting entry. Regulation of rates, practices, and entry into the industry was thought to be the best way to minimize the negative effects of unrestrained competition while encouraging "reasonable" competition and coordination among all modes of transportation and establishing profitable rates and financial conditions within the industry. Entry control was to be accomplished by requiring carriers to hold appropriate authority, issued by the ICC, as a prerequisite to legal operation.

The twin goals of entry control and stability formed the substance of the Motor Carrier Act of 1935. Taken together, they were assumed to lead to the desired end, protection of the public interest. The spirit and founding principles of the Motor Carrier Act of 1935 and the setting in which the act was formulated can perhaps be best summarized in the words of Commissioner Joseph Eastman:

> It is believed that the experience of the past, not only with the railroads but with all industry, and not only in this country but in other parts of the world, shows which course to take.

We relied upon free competition as the means of public protection, and the result was bankrupt and unsafe railroads,
bad labor conditions, flagrant favoritism in rates with the
benefit going to the big shipper and the big community, and
an uncertainty and instability which were demoralizing to
industry in general. Competition was not universal, for the
railroads enjoyed a monopoly at many of the smaller places.
But public regulation was imposed quite as much to cure the
ills of unrestrained competition as to curb the exactions of
monopoly. Of late, the country has begun to discover that
competition can also require restraint in industries which
were not supposed to be affected, like transportation, with
the public interest.[17]

Having abandoned the goal of promoting competition in rail
transportation, the ICC implicitly endorsed a regulatory regime for
trucking with all the shortcomings of its railroad predecessor. Thus,
truck regulation, in imitation of rail regulation, was born into a cartel-
like environment.

Again the theory of wealth-seeking behavior can be applied to
understand the extension of ICC regulation to trucking. Among the
economic benefits sought by interest groups are those that (1) limit
entry or otherwise erect or fortify barriers to entry; (2) give the regulated firm advantages over substitutes and complements; and (3) limit
price competition. As we have seen, the process from conflict to legislation may and often does involve members of the same industry vis-à-
vis each other—large versus small shippers, trunk versus short-line
railroads, and certificated trucking firms versus independent truckers.

Reform of Truck Industry Entry and Rate Regulation: A Case History

On July 1, 1980, the Motor Carrier Act (MCA) of 1980 replaced the
measure that had governed motor carrier regulation for forty-five
years. It did not repeal regulation as some had hoped. Nonetheless it
was a significant step in the direction of deregulation and market-
based competition. The conditions that made the MCA of 1980 possible had been set in motion years earlier. As early as the Kennedy
administration there was support for some form of reduced truck
regulation; every president thereafter (until Carter) tried but failed to
secure passage of reform legislation.

The nonlegislative forces involved in regulatory reform will be
understood more clearly after a preliminary discussion of the administrative (ICC) and legal developments that set the stage. The long-

accepted public convenience and necessity standard used by the commission was first established in *Pan-American Bus Lines Operation*.[18] Under the *Pan-American* criteria an application for new entry was judged on the basis of (1) whether the new operation or service would serve a useful public purpose, responsive to a public demand or need; (2) whether this purpose could and would be served as well by existing lines or carriers; and (3) whether the purpose could be served by the applicant with the new operation or service proposed without endangering or impairing the operations of existing carriers contrary to the public interest. Items 2 and 3 are clearly more concerned with protecting competitors than promoting competition.

The commission's interpretation of the tests was that it had to balance the considerations. The advantages to the public using the proposed service were weighed against the disadvantages, real or potential, to existing service that might result.[19]

The turning point in ICC protection of regulated trucking firms came in *Mayfield Sons Trucking Co. Extension—Kentucky*.[20] In that case, the commission held that the public need might be established by showing the desirability of more competition, a different kind of service, or an improved service. While that interpretation might appear reasonable and balanced, the criteria should be considered in light of the burden(s) the ICC placed on applicants and supporting shippers.

> However, in the final analysis a public need for a proposed service can only be established when the supporting shipper or shippers present sufficient and probative evidence to the commission warranting such a conclusion. In instances such as the one at hand where shippers have not investigated to determine whether protestants' services are indeed inadequate, we will not indulge in an experiment of authorizing additional operations which, though supported by shippers, may jeopardize the very carrier system we seek to improve for the benefit of all shippers.
>
> . . . the Commission favors the existence of sufficient carrier capacity to encourage competition and provide incentives for real innovation and improvement to the public; however, it will not approve the creation of excessive capacity and needless duplication of services which would tend to adversely affect the continuance of efficient operation by existing carriers.[21]

Both *Mayfield* and *Pan-American* required applicants to prove too much. The real effect of the second *Pan-American* criterion (whether this purpose can and will be served as well by existing carriers) was to require the applicant to prove that its own service proposal could not be matched by existing carriers. This requirement was very burden-some. Many protestant (opposing) carriers would not even have been serving the shipper prior to the application proceeding and in any event the protestant carrier had the best knowledge about its own capabilities. Thus opposing carriers were in control of information needed by the applicant to prove its case.

The commission formally removed the burdensome second *Pan-American* criterion in 1979 in Ex Parte No. MC-121, *Policy Statement on Motor Carrier Regulation*. This easing of the applicant's evidentiary burden followed a court challenge to a denial by the commission of authority to operate.

In *P. C. White Truck Lines, Inc.* v. *United States*,[22] the Court of Appeals for the District of Columbia Circuit held that the commission had erroneously based its denial of the application on only one fac-tor—the adequacy of existing service—and had failed to take into account the beneficial effects that increased competition might have on the public. On reconsideration the commission granted the sought authority and inserted language on the potential benefits of increased competition.[23]

This case was much discussed when it appeared. What was gen-erally overlooked, however, was that the commission had ignored its own pronouncements when it decided *P. C. White* the first time. The benefits of competition as a basis for a grant of authority had previously been discussed at great length in, of all places *Pan-American*.[24] The sig-nificance of *P. C. White* is that it reminded the commission that it had to consider competition in application cases or face court reversal.

The commission broke new ground in *Liberty Trucking Co., Exten-sion—General Commodities* (1979):[25] it found (1) harm to a particular carrier to be relevant only if there is a corresponding impact on the public interest, and (2) competition is generally presumed to be in the public interest. The public interest, not competitors' interest, was paramount.

Prior to *Liberty*, a protestant was likely to be successful in keeping out competitors if it could show that it held the proper authority and had transported traffic that a grant would subject to diversion (this assumes the applicant had not proved it would offer a superior ser-vice).[26] The tenor of most past decisions was that the existing carrier should not have its revenues diluted. It was simply presumed that, under the third *Pan-American* criterion, the existing carrier was going to be hurt by new entry.

Liberty required protestants to rebut two presumptions. First, competition is *presumed* to be in the public interest. In essence, the protestant must now contradict the presumption that the grant of authority is good for the public. Second, where previously diminution of revenues was per se injurious to the carrier, now even harm to a carrier became irrelevant unless it affected the public interest. Thus, even the fact that an existing carrier might go out of business entirely would not be controlling unless the protestant could prove that the public would suffer a loss.

The cutting edge of the *Liberty* case is that it shifted determination of the desired level of competition from the regulatory arena to the marketplace. Formerly, the burden of demonstrating that service levels, and by extension competition, were not adequate fell on the applicant. Under *Liberty*, it was the protestants who had to show that it was not in the public interest to grant the authority. Since service, volume, and rates would not likely be affected by any single grant, it became extremely difficult for protestants to show they were adversely affected and, more important, that the public would be hurt by new entry.

The *Liberty* decision was a serious blow to the certificated carrier protestant. The American Trucking Association denounced it and vowed to fight it in court, as indeed it did. Still to be resolved was how harm to existing carriers was to be measured. Was it diversion of the traffic at issue in the application or a more inclusive measure of revenue? The answer came in the *Arrow* decision,[27] in which it was held that "overall traffic" was the relevant measure and that even then it "becomes relevant only when there is corresponding injury to the public."[28] Trucking firms could no longer successfully protest new entry on the grounds that they would lose traffic in a market. Harm had to be measured in overall terms. Even that was merely a threshold test; injury to the public also had to be demonstrated.

The commission was well on its way to dismantling the barriers to entry. Protest standards were tightened so that only carriers participating in the traffic (serving the supporting shipper) could protest. Substantial harm to overall traffic that injured the public also had to be shown. Finally in Ex Parte No. MC-121, *Policy Statement on Motor Carrier Policy* (1979), the commission decided to grant authorities where "applicants for authority show that the service proposed is responsive to a useful public purpose, and that they are fit to perform that service."[29]

Whereas applications for new entry in 1970 were running at about 2,500 per year, by 1979 they were nearly ten times that level. The resources of the commission were being severely strained to process all the new applications; trucking firms were rushing in to take advantage of the new liberalized entry policy. No one knew how long it would last. Critics were saying that the commission had overstepped its authority, and the American Trucking Association and the Teamsters were united in opposition to the commission's new directions.

In part to avoid the need to process many individual applications and in part to identify broad areas where there was need for new authority, the commission created a new operating right—the master certificate—a single certificate issued after a general finding that the public convenience and need would be served by more carriers in a given segment of the trucking industry. The commission staff identified several such segments and issued a report to the commission, which proceeded to conduct rule-making proceedings for the purpose of possibly easing entry requirements in eleven specialized areas of motor carrier transportation. To be explored in each proceeding was the issuance of a master certificate of public convenience and necessity. In some instances contract carriage was also involved.

The MC-135 proceedings were very significant because they involved large segments of the motor carrier industry. Substantive court challenges by the trucking industry in all previous master certification areas had been unsuccessful, the courts noting that individual adjudications were not necessary. The crux of MC-135 was to have been the ability of the commission to develop an adequate record—a difficult task in view of the broad complexities of the subject areas. Meanwhile, the commission was busy on a number of other fronts, the most important of which was approval of rate bureau agreements.

Since 1948, ICC-approved rate bureaus have enjoyed antitrust immunity for collective rate making. Collective rate making is essential to the successful operation of the trucking cartel. Thus, when the ICC began to review rate bureau agreements more closely and hinted at new requirements for approval, it sent shock waves deep into the trucking industry. Perhaps this more than anything else was responsible for the "Fall Offensive of 1979," in which the American Trucking Association and the Teamsters sought to reverse regulatory reform at the ICC.

Beginning in 1972 the commission became increasingly active in ensuring that rate bureaus operated in the public interest. In 1973, the commission instituted a major investigation that resulted in a number of new requirements for approval of the agreements. Perhaps most important, rate bureaus were not permitted to protest or otherwise discourage independent rate actions of their members. Moreover, each rate bureau was required to conform to specific statutory and administrative requirements. For example, agreements must guarantee that members of the rate bureau have full, free, and unrestrained right to take independent action either before or after any determination arrived at through collective action procedures. These and similar reforms made price-fixing agreements more difficult to maintain and competitive rate setting more likely.

The Railroad Revitalization and Regulatory Reform Act of 1976 enacted into law some of the same conditions on railroad collective rate making that the commission had adopted on its own. In addition, it imposed important new requirements designed to modernize the railroad rate bureaus and foster competition among the railroads. It did so by prohibiting collectively made rates and charges on single-line traffic.

At the end of 1977, the commission instituted a rule-making proceeding to determine whether the restrictions on railroad rate bureaus contained in the 4R Act should be extended to motor carriers. On February 28, 1979, a majority of the commission voted to prohibit collective voting or agreement on single-line trucking rates and to limit the voting on joint-line rates to those carriers that can "practicably participate" in the movement under consideration. The commission indicated that it would define "practicably participate" on a case-by-case basis. The commission also limited discussion of a rate proposal by members otherwise not eligible to vote on that proposal to questions of discrimination.

As in the rail area, the restrictions on truckers' voting on single-line and joint-line rates did not apply to general increases and decreases or to broad tariff changes. The commission also extended the prohibition against rate bureaus' protesting the independently established rates of their member carriers. The prohibition was extended to cover all independently established rates of carriers of the same mode regardless of the manner of tariff publication.

The new requirements represented an effort by the commission to confine the antitrust immunity granted the rate bureaus to those areas where agreements on rates between carriers who are otherwise competitors are a genuine practical necessity—such as an agreement on a general increase or an agreement on joint-line rates among the carriers engaged in joint-line service.

In addition to the new requirements applicable to all nonrail rate bureaus, the commission announced that it was reevaluating existing rate bureau agreements to determine whether they were still necessary and consistent with the statute and the public interest. The announcement that the ICC was "reevaluating" existing rate bureau agreements; the issuance of Ex Parte No. MC-121, *Policy Statement on Motor Carrier Regulation*; the beginning of master certification proceedings; and the decision in *Liberty*, when taken together, were clear signals of an about-face in commission treatment of the trucking industry. Add to this the addition of market-oriented new commissioners, bringing to five (out of eight) the number who could be regularly counted on to support reduced regulation, and the introduction by Senator Kennedy and the Carter administration of the truck deregulation bill and one begins to grasp the magnitude of the challenge facing previously stable and prosperous trucking industry cartels.

The American Trucking Association and the Teamsters are among the best organized and disciplined lobbying groups in Washington. Every congressional district has at least one trucking concern whose owner can be counted on to lobby his representative. Neither the ATA nor the Teamsters are hesitant to engage in direct political activity, supporting friendly politicians and working against hostile ones.[30]

By the fall of 1979 it was clear that something had to be done immediately if the forces of reform were to be stopped or reversed. A $2 million "war chest" was created to fight deregulation (in reality, reduced regulation). A public relations firm was hired and a blitz of personal calls on congressmen was launched. Senator Howard Cannon, chairman of the powerful Senate Commitee on Commerce, Science, and Transportation, personally addressed a meeting attended by virtually all the sitting ICC commissioners and asked for a moratorium on major proceedings until June 1, 1980, by which time Congress would have acted on truck deregulation. The ICC was told not to "preempt" Congress, not to take administrative action that would limit Congress's options. The commission heard and heeded the chairman of its oversight committee. In a letter to Senator Cannon, however, the commission indicated that after June 1 it would feel free to resume its proceedings if Congress had not acted.

The ATA, the Teamsters, and oddly enough, some shipper groups were elated; the ICC deregulation tiger had been caged. But like the rumors of Mark Twain's death, the joy was premature. The *Arrow* decision was issued in March 1980. The ATA claimed it was a violation of the moratorium agreement. Nothing happened.

By early spring progress toward new legislation was proceeding very slowly. Finally Senators Cannon and Packwood agreed on a draft bill. Senator Packwood, then the ranking Republican, now chairman, of the Senate Committee on Commerce, Science, and Transportation, provided the Republican votes to produce 10-9 majorities on crucial sections of what was a liberalized entry, procompetitive measure; it embodied Ex Parte No. MC-121, replacing the public convenience and necessity requirement for permanent authority with the more liberal standard that entry serve a useful public purpose responsive to public demand or need. The bill was approved overwhelmingly by the Senate.

In the House things were going even more slowly. A bill more to the liking of the industry was introduced but later withdrawn after heavy White House lobbying and very negative press reception. The Senate bill was later introduced in the House. Attempts to amend it to remove or blunt the more procompetitive sections on entry and rate making were met with Senate firmness and veto threats.

What the industry had hoped would be legislation to check the ICC reforms was instead turning out to ratify much of what the commission had done administratively. This was important because it mooted court challenges to the *Policy Statement on Motor Carrier Regulation* (Ex Parte No. MC-121) and the proceeding on intercorporate hauling. The Motor Carrier Act of 1980 provided for the end of collective rate making in the area of general rate increases by 1984 and generally gave legislative endorsement to commission moves to save fuel, remove gateway restrictions, and broaden grants both in terms of geography and commodities. It also established a zone of rate freedom. The House essentially agreed with the Senate bill in late June and it was signed by President Carter on July 1 in a ceremony full of symbolic and substantive rhetoric (it was a presidential campaign year).

This legislative success for regulatory reform was possible in large part because it was widely believed that in the event legislative efforts failed, the ICC would resume its procompetitive behavior. Having to choose between a Congress that would enact limited reform and an ICC thought likely to press for even greater reform and perhaps deregulation, the industry rallied behind Congress and presented a good face in telling its constituents what a great victory it had won.

Regulatory response is the product of many forces. Through their review of agency decisions, the courts exert a powerful influence. It was a court remand in *P. C. White* that forced the commission to reexamine its position with respect to the *Pan-American* criteria. Meanwhile, a change in the organizational structure of the commission replaced narrow jurisdictional divisions (operating rights, rates, and finance) with general divisions. This removed the influence of powerful division chairmen. The institution of a permanent chairman instead of a rotating one focused responsibility for leadership and made possible an accountable administrative and professional staff. One cannot know for sure how the deregulation of the airlines affected perception and thinking in other agencies, but at a minimum it got people's attention at the ICC.

Summary and Conclusion

The Motor Carrier Act of 1980 and the Staggers Rail Act (also of 1980) constituted major victories for procompetitive forces within the Congress, the Carter administration, the ICC, and the public at large. Unlike the Motor Carrier Act the Staggers Act was widely supported by the railroad industry. Indeed, the railroads had come to the conclusion that continued rigid regulation of the industry would not serve their own long-term interests. The competitive growth of rival modes, particularly trucking, was eroding the railroads' market share of agricultural and manufactured commodities. Railroads were more than willing to surrender some of their collective rate-making protection for greater rate freedom, easier abandonment of unprofitable lines, and a more liberal policy toward mergers and consolidations. Changing technology and the interstate highway system had effectively rendered the ICC-administered railroad cartel impotent.

As Thomas Gale Moore has shown, trucking firm owners and Teamster union employees reaped huge benefits from federal regulation.[31] Earlier ICC rulings that had been made in an attempt to "balkanize" the industry and protect it from competition were being overturned by new ICC decisions on entry, rate bureau activity, intracorporate hauling, dual operations, and the proposals for master certification. The ATA and the Teamsters tried to hide behind many public interest arguments—lost service to smaller communities, rises in freight rates, the common carrier obligation to serve, and highway safety. But these self-serving arguments proved to be unsupported by the evidence.[32]

Trucking is an inherently competitive industry; entry costs are low, significant economies of scale have not been found, and small and medium firms compete successfully with much larger ones. The interests of the public are not served by restrictive entry practices or by rate-making practices that elevate prices above competitive levels. The entry and rate reforms of the 1980 Motor Carrier Act have yet to be fully exploited. Lower freight volumes, a result of the recession of 1980–1982, have not permitted full exploitation of the many new service/rate options possible. But already substantial benefits have accrued to the shipping public.[33]

Notes

1. See George W. Hilton, "The Consistency of the Interstate Commerce Act," *Journal of Law and Economics*, vol. 9, no. 3 (October 1966), pp. 87–113, especially pp. 87–99.

2. Hilton, "The Consistency of the Interstate Commerce Act," p. 100.

3. Stanley Reiter and Jonathan Hughes, "A Preface on Modeling the Regulated United States Economy," *Hofstra Law Review*, vol. 9, no. 5 (Summer 1981), pp. 1393–96, nn. 32, 33.

4. Hilton, "The Consistency of the Interstate Commerce Act," p. 100, and F. M.

Scherer, "Public Regulation Economics Then and Now," prepared for the commemoration of the 100th year of the University of Michigan's Economics Department, 1980 (Department of Economics, Northwestern University, 1980, mimeographed), pp. 9, 11–20.

5. Hilton, "The Consistency of the Interstate Commerce Act," p. 101.

6. Ibid., p. 103.

7. Ibid., p. 104.

8. Sam Peltzman, "Toward a More General Theory of Regulation," *Journal of Law and Economics*, vol. 19, no. 2 (August 1976), pp. 211–40.

9. Hilton, "The Consistency of the Interstate Commerce Act," pp. 104–5.

10. George J. Stigler, "The Theory of Economic Regulation," *Bell Journal of Economics and Management Science*, vol. 2, no. 1 (Spring 1971), pp. 3–21, and Peltzman, "Toward a More General Theory"; the theory of rent-seeking behavior was first advanced by Anne O. Krueger, "The Political Economy of the Rent-Seeking Society," in James M. Buchanan and Roger Tollison, eds., *Towards a Theory of the Rent-Seeking Society* (College Station: Texas A&M University, 1980), pp. 51–70.

11. 182 ICC 263 (1932).

12. Emergency Railroad Transportation Act, 1933, chap. 91, 48 Stat. 211 (1933).

13. Ibid.

14. Regulation of Transportation Agencies, *Second Report of the Federal Coordinator of Transportation*, 73d Cong., 2d sess., 1934, S. Doc. 152 (hereinafter cited as *Second Coordinator's Report*). An account of the report's preparation and of the early days of ICC motor carrier regulation will be found in the comments of Charles S. Morgan in Senate Committee on Commerce, *An Evaluation of the Motor Carrier Act of 1935 on the Thirtieth Anniversary of its Enactment*, 89th Cong., 1st sess., 1965, Committee Print, pp. 4–18.

15. *Coordination of Motor Transportation*. 182 ICC 263, pp. 371–72; *Second Coordinator's Report*, pp. 21, 31, 177; *Congressional Record*, vol. 29 (1935), p. 5653 (remarks of Senator Wheeler).

16. *Second Coordinator's Report*, p. 192. The reference to "stabilization" evokes recollections of Hilton's critique of the goals of early ICC railroad regulation.

17. *Second Coordinator's Report*, p. 96.

18. 1 M.C.C. 190, 203 (1936).

19. *All American Bus Lines, Inc., Common Carrier Application*, 18 M.C.C. 755, 780 (1939).

20. 108 M.C.C. 651, 565–657 (1969).

21. Ibid.

22. 551 F.2d 1326 (1977).

23. 129 M.C.C. 1 (1978).

24. Ibid., at pp. 208–10.

25. 131 M.C.C. 573.

26. Even until the early 1970s, it was common practice to deny applications where the protestant merely held the authority. In most cases, the other issues were neutral. Applicants pretty much provided the same type of service as protestants, and in most cases, shippers did not have complaints of service inadequacy. The most often used language in denying applications was that existing motor carriers should normally have the right to transport all the traffic they can handle adequately, efficiently, and economically, without the added competition of a new operation.

27. *Arrow Transportation*, MC-2862 (Sub-No. 62) F, 133 M.C.C. 941–43 (1980).

28. *Arrow Transportation*, p. 943.

29. Ibid., p. 1.

30. This behavior is consistent with the models in Stigler, "The Theory of Economic Regulation," and Peltzman, "Toward a More General Theory."

31. Thomas Gale Moore, "The Beneficiaries of Trucking Regulation," *Journal of Law and Economics,* vol. 21, no. 2 (October 1978), pp. 327–43.

32. Testimony of Marcus Alexis, acting chairman of the Interstate Commerce Commission, before the Subcommittee on Surface Transportation, House Committee on Public Works and Transportation, on the Motor Carrier Act of 1980, June 10, 1981. See also Moore, "The Beneficiaries of Trucking Regulation," and Andrew F. Daughety, "Regulation of Groups of Firms: The Case of the Operating Ratio in Trucking" (Transportation Center, Northwestern University, February 1981).

33. Alexis, Testimony.

An earlier version of this paper was published as, "The Applied Theory of Regulation: Political Economy at the Interstate Commerce Commission," in *Public Choice* 39: 5–27, Papers from a conference on the Political Economy of Regulation held at Carnegie-Mellon University, May 1–2, 1981.

8

Deregulation and Vested Interests: The Case of Airlines

ALFRED E. KAHN

Regulation as a Creator of Vested Interests

Whenever the government intervenes in the economy in one way or another—whether by spending, taxing, authorizing exemptions and deductions for tax purposes, or guaranteeing loans—it typically confers benefits on some groups of people and, directly or indirectly, burdens on others. In so doing, it necessarily creates vested private interests in a continuation of that particular activity. The interests usually antedate the government action and provide part of the political motivation for the government's undertaking it in the first place; but the explicit intervention by the government then validates those interests, confers those benefits, and makes the beneficiaries eager to see the activity continued.

This generalization applies, of course, to the government's ventures in economic regulation, as well as to its direct budgetary decisions. It is not pejorative but a simple statement of fact. In itself, it does not rule out the possibility that economic regulation will typically be supported also by disinterested parties and undertaken in the expectation that it will serve the public interest as well. Nor, of course, does it demonstrate that any particular act of economic regulation is socially desirable or undesirable.

At the same time a knowledge of who are, or believe themselves to be, beneficiaries of a particular regulation and who are on balance disserved by it is necessary to understanding and evaluating it. And while in principle the special interests of the various parties arguing for or against particular regulatory policies are irrelevant to the merits of their contentions, knowledge of those interests can, in a world of imperfect knowledge, provide us with assistance in evaluating those contentions.

This is by no means to argue that the contentions of parties with private interests in the outcome of a regulatory issue are not worthy of objective consideration. On the contrary, the interested parties are likely to be an invaluable source of the raw material for the making of good public policy. The fact remains, however, that it is usually helpful also to know the private interests of the several parties engaged in debates about what policies will best serve the public interest.

One other pertinent characteristic of economic regulation is that it typically involves some curtailment of competition. Often this intention is explicit: for example, when it is believed that unregulated competition in a particular industry would prove to be destructive, or when the desire is, precisely, to protect domestic companies from the competition of imports. At other times, the suppression or curtailment of competition may be merely ancillary to the principal purpose. When the government regulates public utilities, for example, its principal purpose is to prevent monopolistic exploitation of consumers; at the same time, the underlying conception that monopoly is the most efficient form of organization of such industries usually results in the government's conferring on the utility companies franchises that exclude competitors from their assigned service territories. This will often be the case, again, when regulation is employed to ensure the provision of some particular service to areas or classes of customers whom it might not otherwise be profitable to serve. In this case, the government will protect the utility company from competition in its profitable markets, most often by restricting the entry of firms attracted by the high profits earned there, in exchange for a requirement that it also serve unprofitable ones.

Thus, each of these three main occasions for economic regulation—the belief that unregulated competition would be destructive of some social purpose, the belief that the market in question is a natural monopoly, and the desire to institute or preserve a regime of internal subsidization—usually involves some limitation or suppression of competition. And that kind of governmental restraint naturally both serves the interest of some private parties and gives rise to an interest on their part in its perpetuation.

The beneficiaries of regulation may well be the companies that are subjected to regulatory constraints—restricted in their ability to cut prices in order to take business away from a competitor, or in their ability to extend the scope of their operations to embrace commodities or markets other than the ones authorized by their franchises or certificates—because that limitation on their freedom is part of an industry scheme that protects them similarly from such competition by others. The trucker whose certificate limits him to hauling a specified category of commodities over specified routes can himself be subjected to competitive challenge only if the challenger can persuade a regulatory agency that the additional service is required by the "public convenience and necessity"; the railroads, limited in the rates they may charge, are also insulated from the price competition of truckers, whose proposed rate reductions must receive the approval of a regulatory agency that construes its obligation as one of assuring a "fair" distribution of the traffic between alternative transportation modes.

Or the beneficiaries may be competitors who are *not* themselves thus confined but who enjoy the benefits of the restrictions imposed on their actual and potential competitors—the domestic manufacturers whose products are protected by import restrictions, the local broadcaster previously protected by FCC regulations limiting the ability of cable companies to import broadcast signals into his territory, the obstetricians protected by restrictive state licensing laws from the competition of midwives.

Sometimes the value of that interest in the regulatory curtailment of competition has a clear, objective measure—the value that the market puts upon an operating certificate when some company that does not have one pays the one that does in purchasing the latter's business, or for the temporary loan of the license. When a trucker, after having made a delivery exempt from ICC regulation—for example, of agricultural commodities—faced making the return journey with an empty truck, he would normally surrender 25 percent to 30 percent of his gross revenues on the return trip in exchange for the loan of an operating license from a certificated carrier; and an entrant into the taxicab business in New York City might pay the $10,000 or $15,000 for the cab and another $60,000 for the medallion that conveys the right to engage in the business.

Since the essence of free competition is the right to enter a market without permission from a governmental agency, or upon a demonstration of nothing more than fitness, ability, and willingness to provide the service, deregulation causes the value of these operating rights to decline toward zero.

In these circumstances, understandably, proposals for deregulation—without exception to my knowledge—elicit widespread predictions of undesirable, indeed catastrophic, consequences: (1) deterioration in the quality of service; (2) the loss of service to small towns or rural communities; (3) widespread waste and inefficiencies; (4) epidemics of inebriation (a prediciton that almost always accompanies proposals to eliminate compulsory retail price maintenance in the sale of alcoholic beverages); or (5) creation of a monopoly (paradoxically, since the proposal is to remove governmental restraints on competition).

134

The fact that these predictions are frequently made by beneficiaries of the regulations whose removal is under consideration does not, of course, serve in itself to demonstrate that they are invalid. It is equally axiomatic, however, that disinterested observers and framers of public policy should regard them with skepticism, applying to them rigorous tests of logic and experience.

Airline Regulation: The Players

The policy of domestic airline regulation and subsequent deregulation provides a persuasive illustration of all these generalizations. Beginning with the Civil Aeronautics Act of 1938 and continuing with the Federal Aviation Act of 1958, a pervasive regulatory scheme controlled the development of domestic air transportation until October of 1978. At that time, passage of a deregulation bill completely reversed the policy of regulatory control.

What were the essential elements of that control? Chief among them, regulation through the Civil Aeronautics Board (CAB) controlled the number of major air passenger carriers and the specific routes each airline could fly. The CAB controlled entry into any and every market between two cities, whether by existing carriers or new ones. And for the most part it exercised that authority restrictively. From 1938 to 1976, it did not certify a single new trunk carrier.[1] And, for five or six years in the early 1970s, the Board refused as a matter of policy to entertain any applications for new route authority.

In addition, the CAB fully regulated air fares and exercised some control over quality of service. In some respects, these were less important than control of entry. Wave after wave of new and faster aircraft with lower operating costs kept downward pressure on fares and improved the comfort of air travel—although, as more recent experience demonstrates, regulation clearly discouraged innovative pricing, and in particular the offer of a greater variety of price/quality options. Moreover, essentially unregulated competition among the certificated carriers in scheduling and in the quality of service they offered generally brought costs into line with CAB-determined fares on all types of routes—upward toward the prescribed fare levels in the markets where those fares were set above standard costs, downward, with skimpy services, where the fares would otherwise have been unremunerative.

Through exercise of its authority—including the authority to provide direct dollar subsidies—the CAB ensured the provision of at least minimal adequate service to many smaller cities, at fares lower than would otherwise have been possible.[2]

This scheme of regulation created vested private interests among at least four groups:

1. the major certificated air carriers themselves, who enjoyed the benefit of regulatory insulation from some kinds of competition—and profited thereby (it was this insulation from competition that made their operating certificates valuable and gave them the assurance that even if they could not make a profit, some other carrier would be happy to acquire or merge with them, in order to inherit those certificates)

2. employees, who, through collective bargaining, could divert some of the benefits of suppressed competition to themselves, in the form of higher wages and fringe benefits

3. the smaller cities who were receiving subsidized air service, and

4. airport operators, who could most easily raise capital on the security of long-term leases with established, licensed carriers

Not surprisingly, then, members of these four groups accounted for the bulk of the opposition to deregulation. For example, in the 1977 Senate hearings,[3] most of the major air carriers and all of the witnesses representing labor unions testified in opposition (see tables 8–1 and 8–2). The few exceptions among the carriers were the ones that had been especially constrained by regulation. Pan American Airways had been blocked from domestic service by the CAB; it saw deregulation as offering it the opportunity to enter those markets. Pacific Southwest, an aggressive competitor within California, was looking for an opportunity to move into interstate markets. United Airlines, as the largest domestic carrier, felt that it had been disproportionately prevented by the CAB from entering additional markets and that it was particularly well situated to prevail in full, unrestricted competition.[4]

Witnesses for various localities were divided (see table 8–3): some felt tight CAB limitations on entry had left them in the shadow of big neighboring hubs and that deregulation would bring them more service (for example, Tampa and Oakland); others feared losing service. But even the former sought assurances that present services would not be withdrawn.

The Predicted Dire Consequences of Deregulation

The arguments of these various parties against deregulation focused on six main (and not necessarily mutually consistent) themes. First was the prediction that it would produce gross inefficiency. New carriers would flock into the industry, existing carriers would invade one another's markets, and the sky would be filled with planes flying

TABLE 8–1
AIRLINES TESTIFYING FOR/AGAINST AIR TRANSPORT DEREGULATION IN 1977

Basically for	Basically against
Pan American Airways	Air Transport Association
United Airlines	American Airlines
Others:	Braniff
Aeroamerica	Continental Airlines
Air Wisconsin	Delta Air Lines
Cochise Airlines	Eastern Airlines
Pacific American Airlines	National Airlines
Pacific Southwest Airlines	Northwest Airlines
Cargo Carriers:	TWA
Federal Express	Western Airlines
Flying Tigers	Association of Local
Pinehurst Airlines	Transport Airlines:
Summit Airlines	Air Midwest
	Air New England[a]
	Alaska Airlines
	Allegheny Airlines
	Aloha Airlines
	Frontier Airlines
	Hawaiian Airlines
	Hughes Airwest
	North Central Airlines
	Ozark Air Lines
	Piedmont Airlines
	Reeve Aleutian Airways
	Southern Airways
	Texas International Airlines
	Wien Air Alaska

a. Air New England also presented separate testimony in which it did not oppose deregulation.
SOURCE: U.S. Senate, Committee on Commerce, Science, and Transportation, *Regulatory Reform in Air Transportation*, March 1977.

half-empty (or, presumably, worse, since the average load factors of all certificated carriers had hovered in the 50–55 percent range since 1960). The result would be wasted fuel and excessive promotional expenditures. In short, the introduction of unregulated competition would tend to raise—not lower—operating costs and, therefore, fares.

The second theme was that deregulation would lead to market dominance and control by a few carriers. The major carriers would use

TABLE 8–2
Labor Unions Testifying for/against
Air Transport Deregulation in 1977

Basically for	Basically against
	Airline Pilots Association
	Association of Machinists and Aerospace Workers
	Brotherhood of Railway and Airline Clerks
	Flight Engineers International Association
	International Brotherhood of Teamsters
	Transport Workers Union of America

Source: U.S. Senate, Committee on Commerce, Science, and Transportation, *Regulatory Reform in Air Transportation,* March 1977.

their control of hub airports and established networks (which would enable them to feed continuing passengers on to their own planes), deep pockets for promotion, and surplus or underutilized aircraft to take over an ever-increasing share of the market.

Third, they predicted, service to small communities and on thin routes would disappear. Deregulation would make internal subsidization unsustainable, because vigorous competition would dry up the sources of subsidy—the supernormal profits on the dense, longer routes. The vital link in the national network—scheduled transportation for smaller communities—would be severed.

Fourth, employees would be subjected to great insecurity. For example, new carriers could be organized, using nonunion employees; the advantage this would give them in competition with the established carriers would lead to the loss of hundreds, perhaps thousands of jobs.

Fifth, unbridled competition would jeopardize the safety of airline operations because the pressures it would exert on the carriers to cut costs would tempt them to skimp on maintenance and similar safety-related activities.

Sixth, deregulation would endanger the financial health of the airline companies and so diminish their ability to finance the acquisition of new aircraft. The uncertainty and instability introduced by competition would discourage the financial community from investing in airlines. And this at a time when carriers needed badly to

TABLE 8-3
STATE AND LOCAL ORGANIZATIONS TESTIFYING FOR/AGAINST
AIR TRANSPORT DEREGULATION IN 1977

Basically for	Basically against
American Association of State Highway and Transportation Officials, Standing Committee on Aviation	Airport Operators Council International
	American Association of Airport Executives
Greater Peoria Airport Authority	Conference of State Departments of Transportation
Greater Rockford Airport Authority	
Port of Oakland	Four Corners Regional Committee
Sullivan County, N.Y.	National Conference of State Legislatures
Tampa (city government)	National Governors Conference
	Port of Seattle

SOURCE: U.S. Senate, Committee on Commerce, Science, and Transportation, *Regulatory Reform in Air Transportation*, March 1977.

modernize their fleets by purchasing aircraft that were more fuel efficient and less noisy.

Finally, the argument ran, the industry was already providing good service at declining real prices; what need was there to deregulate: "if it ain't broke, don't try to fix it." Indeed, real fares had generally fallen throughout the industry's history. Even in the 1970s, in the face of a sharp increase in fuel costs, yields—airline revenues per passenger mile—had at worst simply kept up with economy-wide inflation. The existing system of regulatory oversight had created a strong integrated national system, which deregulation and competition could at best only hope to match.

The Competitive Alternative

It would be difficult to quarrel directly with the foregoing characterization of what the airline industry in the United States had achieved by 1977–1978. But its defense of the status quo missed the point of deregulation.

The pertinent question was not whether the performance of the airline industry as of the middle 1970s was "satisfactory," in some absolute sense. It was, rather, how that performance—after forty years of systematic sheltering from competition—compared with the results that might have been or would be achieved if the industry were instead opened to competition. And while a disinterested observer

139

could find, in the industry's actual performance, indications of how it would differ if the restraining hand of government were lifted—in the behavior of unregulated intrastate markets and of the unregulated commuter airlines; in inefficient operations and fare structures—the essence of the case for competition is the impossibility of predicting most of its consequences. The superiority of the competitive market over governmental determinations is the positive stimuli it provides for constantly improving efficiency, innovating, and offering consumers a diversity of choices. It is precisely because neither the government nor industry planners are capable of envisioning the ideal, potential performance of an industry—how its costs will behave, what innovations it may make, what choices it will offer consumers—that we prefer, as a general public policy, to leave those determinations to the forces of a competitive market.

Performance since Deregulation

Although the experience of the airline industry in the very few years since deregulation has been turbulent and dominated by the doubling of fuel prices, worldwide recession, and the effects of the flight controllers strike, it already abundantly documents the wisdom of this national preference for competition. There has been a fairly dramatic restructuring of the industry. New carriers such as Midway, People Express, and New York Air have entered, serving primarily travelers in local, point-to-point markets; some of them operate with few frills or ancillary services such as baggage handling and interline ticketing but with low costs and low fares. More established, aggressive, previously intrastate carriers like Southwest and Pacific Southwest have extended their services regionally. Several of these carriers have concentrated on previously underused second-tier airport facilities, such as Newark, Love Field in Dallas, Hobby in Houston, and Midway in Chicago.

The differences between the costs of these new, point-to-point carriers and the incumbent trunks are dramatic. By drawing on a large pool of available nonunionized workers and paying markedly lower wages (in the case of the genuinely new companies), by getting much greater productivity out of their labor (for example, using two pilots instead of three in cockpits designed for two and having their pilots put in 65 or 70 flying hours per month instead of 45), by using only one type of aircraft and making more intensive use of planes, and by using less congested airports, these carriers have attained cost levels (as table 8–4 shows) on the order of 25 to 30 percent below their integrated-system rivals. Comparisons of individual carriers show even

TABLE 8-4
OPERATING EXPENSES OF INTEGRATED SYSTEM AND
POINT-TO-POINT CARRIERS BY CATEGORY OF EXPENSE, 1980-1981

Expense Category	Integrated System Expenses per ASM (cents per mile)	Point-to-Point Expenses per ASM (cents per mile)
Flying operations	3.39	2.78
Maintenance	0.79	0.55
Passenger service	0.73	0.42
Aircraft servicing	1.26	0.72
Promotion and sales	1.04	0.58
General and administrative	0.31	0.44
Transport related	0.15	0.05
Depreciation	0.48	0.37
Total expenses	8.15	5.91

NOTE: Based on twelve months ending September 30, 1981. ASM = available seat mile.
SOURCE: Civil Aeronautics Board, *Air Carrier Financial Statistics*, September 1981.

more dramatic differences. As a result, several of these carriers, such as Southwest and People Express, have reported substantial operating profits even during periods when others have registered huge losses.

Meanwhile, "local service carriers," such as USAir and Piedmont, have extended their own networks, realizing the benefits of holding on to their originating traffic rather than turning it over to the trunk carriers at intermediate points. As a result, these carriers as a group have remained profitable throughout the recession, in stark contrast with the trunk lines. At the same time, the latter have extended service around strong hubs to provide on-line service to more air passengers. As a result, the former distinction between trunk and local service carriers has been blurred out of existence—except for the appearance of their income statements. Finally, commuter/regional carriers have extended service to smaller cities, both point-to-point and feeder, often replacing the jets of the trunk or local carriers with smaller aircraft, better adapted to the requirements of these markets in terms of their ability to provide convenient scheduling at tolerable cost.

Costs and Productivity. Deregulation has for other reasons as well clearly contributed to improved efficiency. Under pressure of intensified price competition, the trunks have been forced to bargain hard to get more productivity (as well as wage concessions) from their employees. In addition, all carriers have put more seats in their planes (about 20 percent more overall, as table 8–5 shows), with a consequent reduction in cost per available seat mile. And the industry has filled a greater percentage of those seats: even with declining traffic volumes in 1981 and 1982 and with actual departures of scheduled air carriers still above 1978 and earlier year levels, load factors (the industry's principal measure of capacity utilization) have been maintained at a level substantially above that of virtually every prederegulation year back to 1960 (see table 8–6).

These various developments have clearly enhanced productivity throughout the industry. For example, as table 8–7 shows, output per employee in 1979–1980 was roughly 27 percent higher than in 1973 to 1975 for trunks and almost 40 percent higher for local service carriers. Partly as a result, between the fourth quarters of 1976 and 1981, while the price of a weighted bundle of airline inputs rose 105 percent (fuel prices alone went up about 230 percent) average fares rose only 51 percent: while the difference between the two percentages reflects in part the squeeze on profit margins in the latter period, it also reflects a substantial increase in productivity.[5]

Fares. Deregulation was expected to align fares more closely with relative costs. It has. By and large, fares in longer-haul markets and in highly traveled routes have fallen relative to fares in short-haul and thin routes.[6] The result is cost-justified for three principal reasons. First of all, cost per mile declines markedly with the length of the trip because many of the pertinent costs—reservations, ticketing, baggage handling, landing fees—are the same regardless of the length of the trip. Second, cost per seat drops sharply with density: the more the traffic, the bigger the planes that can be used, and there are enormous economies associated with larger planes, increasing up to the limit of the biggest planes available. Third, it is more costly to provide service for business travelers than vacationers. That is to say, it costs more to provide regular scheduled service at convenient times with low load factors—so that one has a reasonable opportunity to get a reservation on relatively short notice—than it does to satisfy discretionary travelers, who can be more readily induced by lower fares to go at one time in very full, big airplanes.

In the light of these cost determinants, fare structures, complex though they may be, have actually become much more rational, not less, since deregulation.

TABLE 8-5

AVERAGE AVAILABLE SEATS PER AIRCRAFT MILE (ALL REVENUE SERVICES), 1971–1981

Passenger Cabin Configuration	1971	1972	1973	1974	1975	1976	1977	1978	1979	1980	1981
Trunks'—domestic operations[a]											
T. fan, 4-eng., wide-bodied	328.6	317.1	328.4	342.4	352.6	356.8	357.4	374.3	378.4	374.5	387.7
T. fan, 4-eng., regular-bodied	133.9	133.3	135.5	141.4	144.3	148.7	150.1	152.6	154.3	167.7	172.7
T. fan, 3-eng., wide-bodied	n.a.	223.7	230.8	233.9	236.3	240.9	246.2	258.6	267.5	268.9	270.8
T. fan, 3-eng., regular-bodied	107.1	107.2	108.5	110.4	112.2	115.4	117.9	120.4	122.2	123.7	129.6
T. fan, 2-eng., wide-bodied	n.a.	n.a.	n.a.	n.a.	n.a.	n.a.	n.a.	230.8	239.9	240.4	242.5
T. fan, 2-eng., regular-bodied	84.5	85.7	87.9	89.5	89.7	90.0	90.5	94.0	95.7	97.8	101.0
Local service—domestic operations											
T. fan, 2-eng., regular-bodied	89.4	89.7	87.4	89.2	89.8	92.0	93.5	94.7	97.7	101.4	—[b]
Turbo-prop, 2-engine	47.4	48.0	47.8	47.8	48.5	48.7	48.3	45.6	46.8	49.3	—[b]

NOTE: n.a. = not available; either no operations were performed with equipment type or group during the period or operations with equipment type or group during the period were too limited for consideration.
a. 1981 figures are for major airlines; they include Republic and USAir.
b. Data no longer collected for this category.
SOURCE: Civil Aeronautics Board, *Aircraft Operating Cost and Performance Report*, 1972–1981.

TABLE 8–6
TOTAL REVENUE PASSENGER LOAD FACTORS
FOR CERTIFICATED CARRIERS AND DOMESTIC
TRUNK CARRIERS, 1960–1982

Year	Total Certificated Carriers (percent)	Domestic Trunks (percent)
1960	59.3	59.5
1961	55.4	56.2
1962	53.0	53.3
1963	53.1	53.8
1964	55.0	55.4
1965	55.2	55.2
1966	58.0	58.5
1967	56.5	57.2
1968	52.6	53.0
1969	50.0	50.3
1970	49.7	49.3
1971	48.5	48.3
1972	53.0	52.4
1973	52.1	51.9
1974	54.9	55.7
1975	53.7	54.8
1976	55.4	55.8
1977	55.9	55.9
1978	61.5	61.2
1979	63.0	63.2
1980	59.0	58.3
1981	58.6	57.3
1982[a]	59.3	58.8

a. For the twelve months ending August 31, 1982.
SOURCES: Data for 1960–1964 are from Civil Aeronautics Board, *Handbook of Airline Statistics*, 1965; for 1965–1971 (col. 1), U.S. Bureau of the Census, *Statistical Abstract of the United States*, 1965 and 1972; for 1965–1971 (col. 2), Robert Kane and Allan Vose, *Air Transportation*, 7th ed. (Dubuque, Iowa: Kendall/Hunt, 1979); and for 1972–1982, Civil Aeronautics Board, *Air Carrier Traffic Statistics*, various years.

Market Deconcentration. Just as efficiency, rather than inefficiency, has emerged with deregulation, so the industry's structure has become less concentrated, not more. The market share of the trunks nationwide has fallen from 92 percent to 83 percent in the short space of four years; and concentration ratios in almost all market categories

TABLE 8–7
PRODUCTIVITY OF SYSTEM TRUNKS AND
LOCAL SERVICE CARRIERS,
1973–1980

Year	Productivity of System Trunks (thousands of RTM per employee)	Productivity of Local Service (thousands of RTM per employee)
1973	77.36	40.33
1974	79.23	41.46
1975	79.75	41.85
1976	86.56	46.05
1977	90.26	48.98
1978	97.75	53.35
1979	103.00	57.80
1980	98.40	56.50

NOTE: RTM = revenue ton-miles.
SOURCES: Data for 1973–1978 are from Civil Aeronautics Board, *Handbook of Airline Statistics Supplement*, 1975, 1977, and 1979; for 1979–1980, Civil Aeronautics Board, *Quarterly Financial Review*, December 1979–1980.

have declined.[7] Several local carriers, rather than being squeezed out of the market, have quickly developed extensive hub-and-spoke[8] route structures that rival those of the major carriers. Perhaps most noteworthy, the value of the operating certificate, enhanced by restrictive regulation, has now fallen to practically zero, as evidenced by the Braniff bankruptcy.[9] Previously, some other carrier would have stepped in to merge with a failing airline—as in the case of Delta and Northeast—in order to acquire its valuable operating rights, thereby foreclosing new entrants from the opportunity to enter the vacated markets.

Quality of Service. What has happened to the quality of service to medium and small cities? It is difficult to generalize, partly because the industry is still in transition, partly because of the disruptive effects of major fuel-price increases, two sharp recessions, and the lingering effects of the air traffic controller strike (all hardly the result of airline deregulation), and partly because there is no simple way of measuring service quality.

Even so—and particularly considering that declining total traffic after 1979 would in any event have resulted in constricted scheduling—the evidence does not seem to reflect a major withdrawal of service to medium and small cities.

First, as recent CAB statistics demonstrate, airports have generally not suffered from a decline in the number of carriers serving them. Virtually the same number of airports received service from *more* carriers as of December 1, 1981, compared with September 1, 1978, as received service from *fewer* (see table 8–8). Second, between November 1977 and November 1979, weekly departures from large hubs increased by about 8 percent, from medium hubs over 25 percent, from small hubs about 4 percent, and from the very small nonhub category of airports about 11 percent.[10] Later declines in traffic—which can obviously not be attributed to deregulation—have reversed those trends. The most recently available data for a period spanning deregulation, June 1978 to June 1982, are shown in table 8–9. Although nonhub departures are down for the period, the decline is only about 12 percent; and departures for the other three categories of cities— large, medium, and small hubs—all show increases over the entire period even though the total traffic was down.

Similarly, Dr. Gary J. Dorman, of National Economic Research Associates, has calculated the minimum number of hours that it took

TABLE 8–8

DISTRIBUTION OF AIRPORTS BY CHANGE IN NUMBER OF
CARRIERS PROVIDING SERVICE,
SEPTEMBER 1, 1978 VERSUS DECEMBER 1, 1981

	Number of Airports
Airports with net increase in number of carriers providing service	229[a]
Airports with no net change in number of carriers providing service	256
Airports with net decrease in number of carriers providing service	221[b]

a. Includes 35 airports not served in September 1978.
b. Includes 121 airports not served in December 1981.
SOURCE: Civil Aeronautics Board, *Report on Airline Service, Fares, Traffic, Load Factors and Market Shares*, no. 22, June 1982.

TABLE 8–9
AIRCRAFT DEPARTURES BY HUB SIZE (48 STATES),
JUNE 1, 1982 VERSUS JUNE 1, 1978

Hub Class	Departures per Week		Percentage Change
	June 1, 1978	June 1, 1982	
Large	60,384	63,825	5.7
Medium	23,076	25,480	10.4
Small	13,788	14,115	2.4
Nonhub	28,575	25,239	− 11.7
Total	125,823	128,659	2.3

SOURCE: Civil Aeronautics Board, *Report on Airline Service, Fares, Traffic, Load Factors and Market Shares*, no. 22, June 1982.

in May 1981, as compared with May 1977, for travelers from a randomly selected sample of fifty (primarily small) cities to get to the central city in their respective regions, put in a six-hour workday and return, along with the corresponding minimum amount of time that it took travelers to do the same thing in the opposite direction. He found that more cities had experienced a substantial reduction in the total amount of time required than had suffered a substantial increase, with an average improvement of nearly an hour.[11] This improvement in service is all the more remarkable considering that the increase in the price of fuel and the decline in total traffic in the interim would almost certainly have tended to produce schedule curtailments, whether or not the industry had been deregulated.

Because of the limited size of his sample and the dispersion of the results, Dorman found that the improvement they showed was not statistically significant; but they did enable him to reject the hypothesis that the quality of service to small cities, as he measured it, had deteriorated, on average.

There seem to be several reasons for these results. First, new and existing commuter carriers have quickly replaced service withdrawn from smaller cities by the major carriers. Second, extension of the hub-and-spoke system by carriers free to fashion their own route structures has made it possible to extend great amounts of on-line connecting service with very few flights. For example, by closely scheduling a bank of twenty incoming flights with an outgoing bank of twenty flights, a carrier can serve 440 city-pair markets, with minimum delay and inconvenience and with only forty departures. In this manner the

TABLE 8–10
AIRCRAFT ACCIDENTS AND FATALITIES, CERTIFICATED CARRIERS, 1971–1982

Year	Aircraft Accidents Total	Fatal	Fatalities	Fatalities per 100 Million Passenger-Miles
1971	41	6	194	0.119
1972	43	7	186	0.100
1973	32	6	217	0.115
1974	42	7	460	0.197
1975	28	2	122	0.065
1976	21	2	38	0.019
1977	17	2	75	0.031
1978	19	4	16	0.005
1979	18	5	352	0.123
1980	15	0	0	0.000
1981	25	4	4	0.001
1982	16	5	235	0.081

SOURCES: Data for 1971–1980 are from Federal Aviation Administration, *FAA Statistical Handbook of Aviation, Calendar Year 1981* (table 9.5), p. 155; for 1981 and 1982, National Transportation Safety Board, Office of Government and Public Affairs, telephone conversation with Brad Dunbar, January 24, 1983.

U.S. air travel network remains open to passengers in most cities and towns. Deregulation has not led to an observable collapse in the network. And there is little reason to doubt that wherever sufficient market demand makes the provision of service economically feasible, an existing or new carrier will provide it.

Nor does the record support the predictions that safety would be impaired. Accidents of certificated carriers and of commuter carriers have not surged; they have fallen. And, while comparisons of fatalities in individual years can obviously be distorted by single large, tragic accidents, the records for 1978–1982 and for 1979–1982, summarized in tables 8–10 and 8–11, were in fact better than average.

The last predicted undesirable effect of deregulation was what it would do to the ability of the industry to finance the purchase of new equipment. New entrants were for a time able to raise capital; more recently the industry's depressed earnings have frustrated several such proposed ventures. An industry that fails to earn an adequate

TABLE 8-11
AIRCRAFT ACCIDENTS AND FATALITIES,
COMMUTER CARRIERS, 1976–1982

| | Aircraft Accidents | | | Fatal Accidents per Million Aircraft- |
Year	Total	Fatal	Fatalities	Miles Flown
1976	38	11	34	0.06
1977	42	9	32	0.04
1978	54	13	47	0.05
1979	57	14	65	0.04
1980	38	8	37	0.04
1981	33	10	36	0.05
1982	21	4	13	0.02

SOURCES: Data for 1976–1980 are from Federal Aviation Administration, *FAA Statistical Handbook of Aviation, Calendar Year 1981* (table 9.12), p. 162; for 1981 and 1982, National Transportation Safety Board, Office of Government and Public Affairs, telephone conversation with Brad Dunbar, January 24, 1983.

return on its existing investment, because it is burdened with excess capacity, is, naturally, likely to be unable to finance the acquisition of new capacity. But that is how the market signals that the new capacity is not needed—for the time being. As demand recovers and/or existing capacity is retired, financial backing should once again be available— although, because of their recent, unfavorable experience, it may well be that the airlines will be more cautious in the future than in the past in modernizing or expanding their fleets. On the other hand, most economists would be likely to blame protective regulation in the past for some part of the industry's present excess capacity.

The record of airline deregulation has not been an unmixed one. The industry has been suffering severe financial hardship—but so have the housing, automobile, and farm equipment industries, as well as the American farmer. Where the industry has suffered, it has clearly been the consequence preponderantly of the general state of the economy, which can hardly be laid at the door of deregulation. What can be attributed to deregulation is a wider variety of service and fare options, lower costs and fares, and an end to barriers to entry. The arguments raised by those with vested interests in the perpetuation of a protectionist regime have proved unfounded. The industry experience since deregulation demonstrates that Congress's rejection of these arguments was justified, as was its expectation that the public interest would be better served by subjecting the industry to the discipline of the free competitive market.

Notes

1. The original sixteen "grandfathered" trunk carriers shrank to ten over that period, as a result of mergers. Local service carriers did not receive permanent certificates until 1955. See, for example, G. Douglas and J. Miller, *Economic Regulation of Domestic Air Transport: Theory and Policy* (Washington, D.C.: Brookings Institution, 1974), pp. 110–13.

2. It is difficult to characterize the extent to which the CAB actually enforced a regime of successful internal subsidization—forcing certificated carriers, protected from competition on their more profitable routes, to provide unremunerative service on thinner routes, to smaller cities. The presence of subsidization is clearly suggested by the following facts: that the downward taper of the CAB-prescribed standard industry fare level (SIFL) with increasing distance was intentionally set less steep than the corresponding taper of costs, with the intention of having the longer flights subsidize the shorter; that, in recognition of this, the Board permitted the local service carriers to set their rates up to 30 percent above the SIFL, with the expectation that the competition of the trunks would prevent them from going up to that level on the longer hauls; that the CAB by no means routinely or automatically permitted the certificated carriers to drop service as they chose; and that the carriers, dependent upon the Board's good will in selecting among applicants for permission to enter new markets, did not feel free to move out of existing markets as they chose (witness the wholesale departures that took place upon deregulation). On the other hand, the minimal service requirements enforced by the Board permitted the carriers to offer correspondingly poor and inconvenient service on unremunerative routes; and in fact the Board permitted the trunks between 1968 and 1978 to drop no fewer than 150 of the points they had been serving—ordinarily delaying the departures only long enough to ensure their replacement by local service carriers, aided by direct subsidy if necessary. At the very least, it seems a fair generalization to say that the extent of genuine, successful internal subsidization—and the consequent threat posed by deregulation to the continued service to small communities—was far less than the advocates of continued regulation claimed.

3. U.S. Senate, Hearings before the Subcommittee on Aviation of the Committee on Commerce, Science, and Transportation, March 21–24, 1977.

4. Among others seeing benefits were the commuter carriers, which were restricted from growing by providing full certificated service.

5. Statistics supplied by the CAB's Office of Economic Analysis. Douglas W. Caves, Laurits R. Christensen, and Michael W. Tretheway find a dramatic improvement in the rate of growth of the industry's total factor productivity in the 1976–1979 period, some four percentage points of which, per year, they attribute to deregulation, as distinguished from such exogenous factors as general recovery in the economy ("Productivity Performance of U.S. Trunk and Local Service Airlines in the Era of Deregulation," Social Systems Research Institute Workshop Series, University of Wisconsin, unpublished, February 1982). Their recalculations, incorporating the 1980 experience, produced substantially different statistical results but did not alter their qualitative conclusion about the beneficial effects of deregulation on airline efficiency/("Airline Productivity under Deregulation," *Regulation*, vol. 6, no. 6 (Nov.–Dec. 1982), pp. 25–28).

One troublesome aspect of these various showings is that they undoubtedly lump under the productivity rubric changes in the nature and quality of the product. Higher load factors and tighter seating configurations clearly mean that the lower unit costs are being obtained by providing poorer service. So long as travelers make the choice freely, the change still means a net improvement in economic efficiency, but it is exaggerated by the physical productivity figures. Moreover, since the average fares referred to in the text are on a per mile basis, a large part of the explanation of the discrepancy between their rise and that of weighted input prices has been the increase in average length of trip: to this extent, again, the favorable performance in average prices would have been the result of a change in product mix, and again, the simple comparison would have exaggerated the welfare improvement.

See also John R. Meyer, Clinton V. Oster, Jr., Ivor P. Morgan, Benjamin A. Berman, Diana L. Strassmann, *Airline Deregulation, the Early Experience* (Boston: Auburn House, 1981), chap. 5.

6. David R. Graham, Daniel P. Kaplan, and David S. Sibley, "Efficiency and Competition in the Airline Industry," manuscript, June 1982.

7. David R. Graham and Daniel P. Kaplan, "Airline Deregulation is Working," *Regulation*, vol. 6, no. 3 (May/June 1982), p. 28.

8. A hub-and-spoke route is a network configuration in which all traffic flows through a central "hub" airport. This provides for extensive on-line connections.

9. By way of contrast, in regulated, international routes, certificates still have considerable value. Pan American offered Braniff $30 million for its South American routes.

10. "Developments in the Deregulated Airline Industry," Office of Economic Analysis, Civil Aeronautics Board, June 1981, p. 53.

11. "Air Service to Small Communities After Airline Deregulation," *N/E/R/A Topics*, National Economic Research Associates, New York, January 1982.

PART THREE

9

Conclusion: Economics, Politics, and Deregulation

The preceding chapters have examined the economic and political factors influencing regulatory policy. Viewed through the lens of economic analysis, much of regulation appears to be a peculiarly cruel hoax. Ostensibly intended to protect citizens against monopoly abuses, threats to health and safety, and degradation of the physical environment, the pure interest-group model of its actual performance implies that instead it is an instrument for protecting well-organized groups against this very public interest. Moreover, because regulation tends to create new special interests whose survival depends on its continuation, deregulation and other regulatory reforms appear least likely to succeed in the very areas where policy has departed most from serving a more general public purpose.

Not surprisingly, the view that regulatory politics is based on special economic interests has led to very cynical conclusions not only about regulatory policy making but also about the overall role of government. Political scientist Murray Edelman has, for example, coined the term "symbolic politics" to apply to a wide range of policies that are justified publicly as serving some broadly based public interest, but that in reality consist of special favors for some small groups.[1] Historian Gabriel Kolko puts the matter even more strongly, interpreting regulatory policies in Marxist terms as straightforward means to protect capitalists from consumers and workers.[2]

Such cynical conclusions do not seem warranted and, most importantly, do not fit the facts, especially since the early 1970s. Although regulation of emissions into the atmosphere by federal, state, and local environmental protection agencies may have erected significant barriers to new competition by the late 1970s, the initial passage of environmental legislation in the 1960s can hardly be attributed to some cynical plan by industry. The very interests that now see value in environmental controls because they are biased in favor of established firms were most vociferous in opposing the laws that now benefit them. Indeed, the switch in positions may well be entirely rational. The cost to established firms of the environmental controls applied to date may well exceed the benefits of retarded entry of new competitors; given the presence of environmental regulation, however, a system biased in favor of incumbent firms appears more attractive to them than a more balanced and more effective one.

Perhaps the most dramatic turnaround in regulatory policy took place in the mid-1970s at the Civil Aeronautics Board. In the early 1970s, the CAB appeared to be oriented solely toward the cartelization of the airline industry. It refused even to process applications by new companies to enter the interstate airline business. It denied standing in regulatory proceedings to consumer interests. It attempted to organize collusive agreements among airlines to reduce service in competitive markets so that airlines could earn higher profits. And it engaged in an almost comical process of trying to cure by regulation the recurrent outbreaks of competition in service amenities, even to the point of writing regulations that defined the size of a coach-class seat and the amount of meat that could lawfully be served on a sandwich.

Within a very short period the CAB completely reversed its policies and adopted a procompetitive regulatory stance. It vastly increased the route-authorities granted to established airlines, allowed new, low-price carriers to enter the industry, and even advocated its own dissolution. Much of this reversal has been attributed to the change in the hierarchy of the agency: the appointment of Alfred Kahn as chairman and Elizabeth Bailey as member, and the acquisition of such key staff people as Darius Gaskins and Michael Levine to oversee the deregulatory process. Although these people certainly played a key role in airline deregulation, the agency had begun its dramatic shift even before they arrived.[3] Since the mid-1960s there were critics within the agency itself who believed that the protectionist policies of the CAB were unwarranted. When the agency began to be severely criticized by academic scholars, the courts, and Congress, it turned to these internal dissidents to produce a report about the problems of the agency and their solutions. The result was a blueprint for turning around the policies of the agency.[4]

A similar dramatic policy reversal took place at the Federal Communications Commission at approximately the same time.[5] For the first thirty years of telecommunications regulation after the passage of the Communications Act of 1934, the FCC regarded interstate telecommunications as a natural monopoly and pursued a policy of protecting the dominant firm, AT&T, from competitive entry. In the late 1960s, however, the FCC in two important cases concluded that a definite boundary between monopoly and competition had to be drawn and that the boundary should be based upon what was most desirable for users of the system. In the Specialized Common Carrier Decision and the first Computer Inquiry, the FCC came to the view that competitors should be permitted if they offered distinct new services; in both cases, however, the FCC affirmed that the heart of the interstate telecommunications system—message toll telephone service—would remain an AT&T monopoly.

These two decisions had unanticipated consequences rather like releasing a genie from a bottle. The prospect of competitive entry, even at the fringes of the industry, attracted a variety of entrants as well as a rich array of competitive (and anticompetitive) responses by AT&T. Within a few years the boundary between natural monopoly and competition became technically and economically indistinct and legally arbitrary. By the mid-1970s, one competitor, MCI, began to offer a service that was equivalent to message toll telephone service. At first, the FCC tried to prevent this service, but the courts took the position that the agency had to develop a positive rationale, based upon objective evidence, that the AT&T monopoly should be protected in the public interest. Rather than attempt to develop this rationale, the agency decided to adopt a policy of regulation by reluctance: competition would be permitted wherever it appeared reasonable and possible, and regulation would be relied upon only where competitors were weak or nonexistent. In the second Computer Inquiry the agency all but eliminated the idea of a boundary between monopoly and competition based upon a technical definition and laid out ground rules for allowing competition to flourish wherever it might arise in all aspects of telecommunications.

The FCC has also recently undertaken a similar leadership role with respect to deregulation of certain aspects of cable television and broadcasting. Its current proposal to repeal its restrictions on network participation in syndication markets is but the latest in this series of reforms.

The cases of these agencies, and of others in the same period, can teach us much about the process of regulatory reform. In these instances the agencies took the lead in deregulating or reforming regulatory policies, anticipating by several years changes in the policies espoused by Congress and the executive branch. Similar stories can be told about the Interstate Commerce Commission's position on trucking and about the introduction of marketlike processes for pollution control by the Environmental Protection Agency. Such stories show that while regulation *can* be responsive primarily to well-represented special interests, it *need not* be. The important question that these stories raise is why agencies resisted the forces of special interests in the mid-1970s and embarked upon a dramatic reevaluation of their own policies.

The interest group view of government processes does not state that well-organized interests always get what they want; it instead predicts which interests can be expected to organize effectively to be represented in decision-making processes. In an environment in which policy makers, whether in regulatory agencies, the executive branch, or Congress, passively respond to requests put before them, special interests can carry the day. This was the difficulty perceived by the Founding Fathers when confronting the problem of constitutional design: how can a governmental system be devised that is responsive to the citizenry but that does not passively allow policy to be captured by factions?

Regulatory agencies prior to the 1970s were often roundly criticized for embodying the kind of government process most susceptible to factions. Having narrowly specialized, targeted responsibilities, they are easily overlooked by most of the citizenry—and often by political leaders in the executive and legislative branches as well. Because they are normally delegated quasi-legislative decision-making authority constrained only by broad, often extremely vague policy mandates, they face the danger of becoming miniparliaments in which only a handful of interests seek representation. And the administrative requirements for bureaucratic policy making impose expensive procedural burdens on agencies, increasing the likelihood that only directly affected interests will find it worthwhile to bear the costs of representation.

Prior to the reforms of the 1970s, the conventional wisdom about regulation was that though political leaders might be sincere in believing regulatory statutes served some diffuse public interest or noble purpose, regulatory agencies had actually evolved into moribund protectors of the very interests they were designed to control. The 1970s witnessed a dramatic reversal of this tendency in a wide variety of agencies. The question is why, and what does this portend for the future of regulatory reform and deregulation?

In the long run, a number of factors militate against a fully captured agency, that is, an agency serving only special interests. One is the protection against it in the constitutional design of the federal government. A fully captured regulatory agency is vulnerable to attack by political entrepreneurs who owe no political debt to the special interests that seek to use an agency for their own purposes. The complicated system of representation in elected federal offices protects against the possibility that a special interest can strongly influence all elected officials. To the extent therefore that an agency becomes moribund and passively responds to a special interest in a manner that injures another segment of the citizenry, the way is opened for a politician to expand his own support by exposing it. An example is the hearings launched in 1974 by Senator Edward Kennedy to investigate the policies and practices of the Civil Aeronautics Board.[6] Another example is the use made of the deregulation issue as a presidential campaign issue by President Carter in 1976 and President Reagan in 1980.

A second element is the continuing scrutiny of regulatory policy by scholars in economics, law, and political science. In each discipline the study of regulatory policy constitutes a separate, developed field of research. The poor performance of several economic regulatory agencies in the period following World War II gave rise to a spate of books and articles by these scholars, providing an intellectual foundation for the work of reformers in the agencies and elsewhere in the government.

A third element is in the nature of government service. There certainly is no direct financial incentive for regulators to operate as efficient cartel managers. Although some have argued that regulatory agencies can act as a revolving door for future employment in regulated industries, such incentives are at best indirect. They tend to apply only to a fraction of an agency's employees and then only at the highest levels. Moreover, a decision maker who responds passively to requests from a client group does not thereby establish credentials as a more active decision maker in the private sector, a position requiring analytical abilities as well as the ability to cause things to happen. In any case, it seems implausible that for a significant period of time all important positions in an agency would be filled by those seeking rewards from regulated industries by passively responding to their every request. Indeed, even before the tumultuous 1970s most regulatory agencies—even the most moribund—had some staff members and commissioners who viewed themselves as independent actors attempting to perform a public service.

Strong evidence supporting this view is the collective and steady effort of agencies to improve their capabilities for internal analysis and to use internal studies and general inquiries for examining important policy issues. A capability for internal analysis is a necessary component of an agency seeking to serve a general public interest—the protection of consumers from monopoly, for example—in a milieu in which only the regulated industry and its most powerful customers are likely to be represented. Such a capability is necessary if an agency is to sift out purely self-interested arguments from all the information made available to it by groups participating in its deliberations and by its own monitoring of the performance of the regulated industry. The FCC's creation of special staff for the network inquiry stands as an excellent example of such independent capability. The analysis conducted by that staff was a basis for the present proposal to repeal the network financial interest and syndication rules, among other reforms.

From these observations we derive a strategy for reforming regulation and protecting against the factionalism deplored by political analysts since the founding of the republic. First, a central element is a continuing focus on the intellectual content of regulatory policy: whom does it affect and how does it affect them? Like the private sector, government is strongly affected by entrepreneurs—people in agencies and in elected offices whose objective, whether arising from political or personal motives, is to be at the forefront of a new political issue oriented toward general rather than special interests. Such actors can be persuaded by the facts; hence the role played by in-house analytical staff and researchers outside the agency is an important one.

Second, another important element is to keep the cauldron of regulatory policy bubbling by making it accessible at low cost to a variety of interests. The value of various types of citizen groups—consumerists, environmentalists, and the like—is not so much that they actually represent accurately a diffuse, heterogeneous general public. That indeed is an unrealistic expectation. More important is that they continue to raise questions about the subtle ways in which regulatory rules may serve narrow self-interest and that they serve as a vehicle for keeping regulatory policy making a government activity carried out in the sunshine of public scrutiny. Just as regulators can make effective use of arguments and information that well-represented private interests provide, so too can they make similar use of the public interest groups. Here also the sifting process should be applied to determine whether the questions raised are valid, and whether the position taken truly represents a general public interest and is intellectually well founded.

The implications of these arguments for the future of regulatory reform are favorable. Many regulatory agencies can now independently perform internal analysis and presumably will continue to do so unless the budgets for these efforts disappear. The Executive Office of the President has also established review of the regulatory processes in the Office of Management and Budget. Even the Congress, by expanding subcommittee staffs and creating strong capabilities for policy analysis in the Congressional Budget Office, the General Accounting Office, and the Office of Technology Assessment, can acquire its own independent assessments of these issues.

The successes of regulatory reforms undertaken since the mid-1970s give further cause for hope. Indeed, one scholar of regulation and participant in deregulation at the CAB argues that the record of the 1970s should cause a revival of the progressivist "public interest" theory of regulation.[7] Because of the reforms begun in the 1970s, a solid history is being constructed to support the view that competitive market forces benefit the general public and that regulation should end or be redirected when it tries to stifle them.

This is not to say that government has no role in channeling and constraining the freewheeling activities of the private economic system. The lesson instead is that incentives are a powerful force for serving the interests of the general public and can be effectively channeled to that end by enlightened, procompetitive regulatory policies. In some cases, this line of reasoning leads to deregulation, as in the case of most communications and transportation sectors. In others, the analysis leads to a change in the way regulation is undertaken. In environmental regulation, for example, it implies a greater reliance on marketable emissions permits, emissions fees, and cost-benefit analysis in setting and attaining environmental objectives.

In our view, recent history provides an important lesson regarding the American experiment with regulation: there ought to be a presumption—open to rebuttal—in favor of competitive market approaches for achieving effective social control of business. Arguments against deregulation based on either a desire to avoid competition or a wish to preserve interests inadvertently created by regulation itself deserve short shrift.

This point deserves elaboration. Economic and technological conditions are changing rapidly, and market competition has usually been the system that has adapted most efficiently to change. But who speaks for the invisible hand? Competition has only a fragile constituency. Regulated businessmen often have everything to gain from regulatory predictability and something to lose—their businesses—from the unpredictability of market forces. The benefits to the public of competition are theoretical and diffuse, but no less real than the benefits of regulation to particular interests. Advocates of continued deviation from the competitive model ought to bear the burden of proof.

The future of attempts to dismantle the excesses of the American experiment with regulation depends on the willingness of policy makers and public alike to understand the economic basis of interest groups. This requires not that we be cynical but that we come to appreciate the perspicacity of the Founding Fathers in designing a system of government that runs on the energy of such groups without being captured by them. The system can run well only if it represents citizens who understand its foundation, its strengths, and its weaknesses, and who insist that their officials be equally well informed.

Notes

1. Murray Edelman, *The Symbolic Use of Politics* (Champaign, Ill.: University of Illinois Press, 1964).

2. Gabriel Kolko, *Railroads and Regulation 1877-1916* (New York: Norton, 1965).

3. Martha Derthick and Paul Quirk, "Why the Regulators Chose to Deregulate," in Roger G. Noll, ed., *Regulation and the Social Sciences* (forthcoming).

4. Civil Aeronautics Board, *Regulatory Reform: Report of the CAB Special Staff* ("Pulsifer Report"), Washington, D.C., 1975.

5. Roger G. Noll, "The Future of Telecommunications Regulation," in Eli Noam, ed., *Regulating New Telecommunications Networks* (New York: Harcourt, Brace, Jovanovich, 1983).

6. Steven Breyer, *Regulation and Its Reform* (Cambridge: Harvard University Press, 1981).

7. Michael E. Levine, "Revisionism Revisited? Airline Deregulation and the Public Interest," *Journal of Law and Contemporary Problems*, vol. 44 (Winter 1981), pp. 179-195.

Contributors

Roger G. Noll is Institute Professor of Social Science at the California Institute of Technology. He is the author of numerous books and articles on regulation, including *Economic Aspects of Television Regulation* (1972), which he wrote with Merton J. Peck and John McGowan.

Bruce M. Owen is an economist in private practice in Washington, D.C. He was formerly chief economist of the antitrust division at the Department of Justice and of the White House Office of Telecommunications Policy. He has taught at Duke and at Stanford universities and is author or coauthor of many books and articles, including *Television Economics* (1974) and *The Regulation Game* (1978).

Marcus Alexis is chairman and professor of economics and professor of urban affairs and policy research at Northwestern University in Evanston, Illinois. He has written widely on regulation, employment discrimination, and the economics of the housing market. He served as commissioner and acting chairman of the Interstate Commerce Commission during the Carter administration.

Andrew S. Carron is a senior fellow of the Brookings Institution in Washington, D.C. He is the author of a number of books and articles on regulation in airline and financial markets, including *The Plight of the Thrift Institutions* (1982).

Robert W. Crandall is a senior fellow of the Brookings Institution in Washington, D.C. He has taught at the Massachusetts Institute of Technology and is the author of a number of books and articles on regulation, including works on the regulation of television and of the environment. He was formerly economic assistant to FCC Commissioner Glen Robinson.

Alfred E. Kahn is Robert Julius Thorne Professor of Economics at Cornell University and is a special consultant to National Economic

Research Associates. He was chairman of the New York State Public Service Commission and of the Civil Aeronautics Board. He also served as chairman of President Carter's Council on Wage and Price Stability and was advisor to the president on inflation.

JOSEPH P. KALT is assistant professor of economics at Harvard University. He has served on the staff of the President's Council of Economic Advisers and as a consultant to the U.S. Department of Energy. He is the author of numerous books and articles on energy issues, including *Petroleum Price Regulation: Should We Decontrol?* (with Kenneth J. Arrow) and *The Economics and Politics of Oil Price Regulation.*

SELECTED AEI PUBLICATIONS

Regulation: The AEI Journal on Government and Society, published bimonthly (one year, $18; two years, $34; single copy, $3.50)

Credit Controls: Should We Revive or Expand Them? (46 pages, $3.95)

Regulating Consumer Product Safety, W. Kip Viscusi (1984, 116 pp., cloth $14.95, paper $5.95)

Ethics-in-Government Laws: Are They Too "Ethical"? Alfred S. Neely IV (1984, 58 pp., $4.95)

The Regulation of Pharmaceuticals: Balancing the Benefits and Risks, Henry G. Grabowski and John M. Vernon (1983, 74 pp., $4.95)

The Political Economy of Deregulation: Interest Groups in the Regulatory Process, Roger G. Noll and Bruce M. Owen (1983, 164 pp., cloth $15.95, paper $7.95)

Nuclear Safety: Risks and Regulation, William C. Wood (1983, 89 pp., $4.95)

Meeting Human Needs: Toward a New Public Philosophy, Jack A. Meyer, ed. (1983, 469 pp., cloth $34.95, paper $13.95)

The Regulation of Air Pollutant Emissions from Motor Vehicles, Lawrence J. White (1982, 110 pp., cloth $13.95, paper $4.95)

• *Mail orders for publications to:* AMERICAN ENTERPRISE INSTITUTE, 1150 Seventeenth Street, N.W., Washington, D.C. 20036 • *For postage and handling, add 10 percent of total; minimum charge $2, maximum $10* • *For information on orders, or to expedite service, call toll free* 800-424-2873 • *When ordering by International Standard Book Number, please use the AEI prefix—0-8447* • *Prices subject to change without notice* • *Payable in U.S. currency only*

AEI ASSOCIATES PROGRAM

The American Enterprise Institute invites your participation in the competition of ideas through its AEI Associates Program. This program has two objectives: (1) to extend public familiarity with contemporary issues; and (2) to increase research on these issues and disseminate the results to policy makers, the academic community, journalists, and others who help shape public attitudes. The areas studied by AEI include Economic Policy, Education Policy, Energy Policy, Fiscal Policy, Government Regulation, Health Policy, International Programs, Legal Policy, National Defense Studies, Political and Social Processes, and Religion, Philosophy, and Public Policy. For the $49 annual fee, Associates receive

- a subscription to *Memorandum*, the newsletter on all AEI activities
- the AEI publications catalog and all supplements
- a 30 percent discount on all AEI books
- a 40 percent discount for certain seminars on key issues
- subscriptions to two of the following publications: *Public Opinion*, a bimonthly magazine exploring trends and implications of public opinion on social and public policy questions; *Regulation*, a bimonthly journal examining all aspects of government regulation of society; and *AEI Economist*, a monthly newsletter analyzing current economic issues and evaluating future trends (or for all three publications, send an additional $12).

Call 202/862-6446 or write: AMERICAN ENTERPRISE INSTITUTE
1150 Seventeenth Street, N.W., Suite 301, Washington, D.C. 20036